RAISE*your*GAME

*How to build on your successes
to achieve transformational results*

I dedicate this book to people who think they can change the world.

You can...

How to build on your successes
to achieve transformational results

RAISE
your
GAME

SUZANNE HAZELTON

ecademyPRESS
www.ecademy-press.com

RAISE*your*GAME
How to build on your successes to achieve transformational results

First published in 2012 by
Ecademy Press
48 St Vincent Drive, St Albans, Herts, AL1 5SJ UK
info@ecademy-press.com
www.ecademy-press.com

Cover design by Michael Inns
Artwork by Karen Gladwell
Author Photograph by Gavin Thorn Photography
Printed by TJ International Ltd, Padstow, Cornwall
Printed on acid-free paper from managed forests.
This book is printed on demand to fulfill orders, so no copies will
be remaindered or pulped.

ISBN 978-1-908746-59-7

Contents

*"How will you know when you've got there if you
don't know where you're going."*

Acknowledgements

"Silent gratitude isn't much use to anyone."

~G.B. STERN

The first thanks goes to you, the reader, for taking the time to explore this book. Please take what's useful to you so that you can find new and different ways to *raise your game.*

Over the years, I've been fortunate to have worked with many inspirational colleagues and to have found mentors who have been influential in developing my thinking. The remainder of this section is a small piece of indulgence to formally thank some of these people; those who have inspired, and those who have supported me through the writing and editing process to get this book published.

I've had some great mentors in my career – and I'd like to thank them for believing in me: Clare Burgum, Christopher Hales, Ruth Jones, Murray Low, and Patrick de Broux. Ashley Bookman has been influential on my thinking. I've worked with a number of associates over the years, those of whom have also provided me with significant food for thought include: Doug Moffat, Nigel Dennis, Ian Blair, Alex Hayward, Nick Dingley, Jan Lancaster, Mo Rye and Miles Peacock. I've had many awesome and inspirational colleagues within IBM – too many to list you all – but thank you.

Those with whom I've worked and have been inspired most recently include: Christine Lissoni, Alison Hoghton, and Louis Larché.

In my advanced study of Psychotherapy – Transactional Analysis (TA), I've studied with and found both Adrienne Lee and Ian Stewart amazing trainers with a wealth of experience and knowledge.

In my studies of Positive Psychology, I've been fortunate to study under Dr Boniwell, Dr Hefferon, Dr Popovic and Dr Thompson – they have incredible academic prowess, and have challenged my thinking and developed my academic rigour. My colleagues on the course have been a superb source of encouragement and positivity.

Thank you too, to all the thousands of people I've trained and coached over the years – I've learned so much from you.

I would like to give special thanks to several people who invested their time to read early drafts of this book, and provided comments and suggestions. Thanks to Lucy Chapman, Darren Sayer, Sarah Ramsey, Ian Christelow and Mike Clark.

I would also like to thank Mindy and the team at The Book Midwife for their editing and design efforts.

Thanks to my many friends who've supported me in many ways through this process.

I'd also like to publically thank my parents for their on-going encouragement to do "whatever makes you happy".

Finally, thanks to my partner Angus Lyon for his continued love, support and encouragement. His thoughts, comments and feedback were invaluable during the writing process.

Introduction

"It is in the moment of your decisions
that your destiny is shaped."

~ ANTHONY ROBBINS

About twenty years ago I started out on a quest to raise *my* game. For the past ten years I've worked extensively to assist others to raise theirs. I've consolidated what I've learned, so that you can benefit from two decades of experience, and a framework that I use with my clients that integrates the best from a number of different development fields.

Been there, done that, got the t-shirt

This book is written for the business owner already familiar with success, who has started to notice the beginnings of being 'stuck in a rut'. Something that's not often discussed is that success can bring boredom – not boredom that comes from doing nothing, but the boredom of not having a challenge – the mindless repetition. Boredom is a waste of your creative energy and can be a factor in depression. You may not be aware that you're bored, but *something* has motivated you to pick up the book and consider your next challenge. *Raise your game* will help you identify what you can change, set your vision for what you want, and give you a process for making incremental changes to achieve your next level of success.

Perhaps you're waiting for forces outside of your control to instigate a change. Are you waiting for the economy to pick up? Until then, you're biding time. Or marking time? I'll encourage you to put your plans in place and start taking steps towards achievement.

Challenge

The challenge you set yourself has to be significantly larger than anything you've achieved up until now, and has to be congruent with who you are and what you stand for to ensure that you are motivated by it. I suggest that the challenge that you set yourself is an order of magnitude larger than you've successfully achieved before − if you're going to be committed to something − make it worthy of your investment of time and energy. Setting this challenge will contribute to you raising your game and achieving transformational results. Ensure the challenge is something that excites and invigorates you.

Transformational Results

Achieving transformational results won't just benefit you; They will transform the lives of others around you, perhaps by providing more jobs or opportunities, or by providing a better service or product. Because of your big goals, your proven success at achieving transformational results will lead to you living life very differently to the way you live today. I suggest it could be an order of magnitude − different − yet in a positive direction.

People often define success in comparative terms, as in "more successful than ..."; however, each of us has a different nuance of specifically what success means to us. I'll encourage you to define what success means to you. My personal belief is that we can each be successful; the more successful we are as individuals, the more the institutions and communities around us will thrive.

Learning from mistakes

With my experience of training and coaching literally thousands of people, I've seen (and made) many of the common mistakes that people make. Forewarned is forearmed as they say. The book highlights over 55 common mistakes that people make when trying to raise their game. These mistakes, and tips to avoid them are included so that you can learn from other people's mistakes to put you on the fast-track for achieving transformational results. I realise that it's not always possible to learn from observing others. For example I don't think it would be easy to learn to ride a bike just from observing the mistakes of others – but I do think that having an awareness of what common mistakes are, can fast-track our learning. This is because we can seek to avoid the mistake, or if we find we've made it we can quickly acknowledge it and move on.

Overview

This book covers a broad range of topics relating to your personal development. Having worked with many business owners, I recognise that reading doesn't always make it to the top of the 'to-do' list. If you only read one business or development this year, then make it this one. The book touches on different topics and provides you with many different practical activities that you can use immediately to raise your game.

What you will see is that you don't have to make big changes to get a massive impact. If you're open, learning can be gained from even the simplest of situations. Read this book in small sections, and then put the activities into practice and you will notice the improvement in your results.

The numbers in the text refer to a bibliography at the end of the book – which most of you will glide over – but if you're inspired to learn more on the topic, the reference section will give you a place to start.

Chapter 1 acknowledges the successes you've had already, and recognises that this successful place can become a bit too comfortable and, like a low squashy sofa, can take a bit of effort to raise yourself from. This chapter focuses on the downside of achieving your goals. I'll explore the research around creating a fulfilling life and introduce three different ways to tackle boredom.

I start the process of exploring how the way we think about the world may be holding you back. The book will take you on a journey of change; however, you are in control of what to change and when to change it. You may not be ready to make changes immediately but when you are ready to embark on this journey, this book provides power tools and proven approaches to break free of limitations and constraints.

There's a widely held belief that keeping your options open is a good thing, I suggest that options can hold you back. I challenge you to commit to a single course of action – to be absolutely clear as to where you are heading while monitoring results – then having the ability to make adjustments as required. By being more focused you will achieve more.

Why don't people make positive changes in their life more often? Perhaps you too have started something and it became too difficult so you gave up. In Chapter 2, I show you the phases of change that will enable you to put strategies in place to be successful, and you'll see that you need different support strategies at different stages. The ups and downs of change form predictable cycles that you can plan for, ensuring you have the right support. Athletes may run the race alone, but they generally have a large 'home team' in the background supporting them. Coaches, nutritionists, physiotherapists and sports massage therapists – they don't achieve this alone.

Having explored that change has its ups and downs, Chapter 3 explores how you can ensure you have a 'resilient mental attitude'.

Such an attitude will support you, especially through the 'downs', and enable you to become increasingly aware of opportunities all around. This chapter looks at something called 'mindset'. It's about having the right attitude for success. There are two distinct mindsets; the fixed and growth mindset. We don't all have a mindset for success in all situations, so I give you some tips for how to notice which mindset you're using and be able to switch into your growth mindset at will.

With a growth mindset, you'll see situations differently; you'll even begin to notice new opportunities. Let me give you an analogous example. When I was around seven years old, I was found to be (very) short-sighted. I remember leaving the opticians having received my first pair of glasses, and exclaiming: "Wow! Look, there are words everywhere." Of course the 'words' had always been above shops and on the side of buses – indeed 'everywhere' – just I'd never been able to see them. In a similar vein, a fixed mindset will stop you seeing opportunities.

Chapter 4 takes a short backward glance at what's brought you this far. I'll encourage you to see what themes link your successes together. There's also time to explore what you have learnt from experiences where the situation didn't go to plan.

Having mined your past for key learnings, and having started the process of understanding your key assets, Chapter 5 is where you start to look forward – to design your vision. This is a very practical chapter with lots of ideas and suggestions for you to carry out, because in my experience people can find this quite challenging. Visions – like bread dough – need time to prove. By the end of this chapter you should have mixed the raw ingredients; developed your vision; cover; set aside and be able to leave in a warm place for a couple of chapters.

Our internal decision criteria: our values, are so pervasive – that most of us are not consciously aware of them. We use our values to make decisions (or they cause us to procrastinate over decisions), in addition our values can cause conflict within ourselves and potentially with others. Our values influence many aspects of our life and can influence the choices that we make. Chapter 6 gives you a process for looking at your values, and discerning their priority. The chapter also introduces the reader to the concept of value clusters, and demonstrates how values change over time. Your values may evolve over time – this is normal – stop resisting!

Implemented consciously, values and vision can massively affect your ability to raise your game; by contrast, Chapter 7 looks at how even small changes can have a big impact. After the 2012 London Olympics, Britain's continued success in the cycling was cited as being because of the 'aggregation of marginal gains'. Additionally, small changes in one aspect of your life affect other aspects: a small stone in your shoe may cause a blister, a blister may cause your posture to be affected and give you backache, and so on. Or to quote Anita Roddick: "If you think small things don't make a difference, you've never been in bed with a mosquito." The positive example may be that drinking more water has a positive effect on our skin, hair and digestion – although in Chapter 8 – I'll explore that negative has a bigger impact than positive.

I also introduce the concept of monitoring your thought patterns. The brain spews out thoughts and most of the time they are unchecked. I'll provide an overview of some thought patterns that can hinder progress. I'll give you a process to take the odd thought off the conveyer belt to randomly sample thoughts – for quality control purpose – to check they're still valid. I introduce the concept of 'provocative change'. These are short-term changes designed to give you an opportunity to develop your awareness, and begin to change the thinking patterns that might be holding you back.

Chapter 8 explores the importance of positive emotions, for building resilience and developing your 'thought-action repertoire' – that's your ability to see and act upon opportunities. In addition to encouraging you to know, and use the 'usual suspects' or the typical approaches you have for lifting your spirits, I'll also introduce a couple of other proven ways to engender positive emotions. Such examples include a bit of mental time travel – all from the comfort of your armchair – or wherever you happen to be!

With your 'positive' kit bag packed and ready to go, it's useful to touch on some of the common fears that hold people back. These fears are experienced by many people, and I want to show you that you don't have to let them hold *you* back. Chapter 9 will give you the confidence to overcome, or at least to sidestep these fears, and get on with the important task of raising your game.

Some people are motivated by 'away from' energy – anything to get away from the situation. I guess this is where the expression *"out of the frying pan into the fire"* comes from – someone so keen to get away they don't care or plan where they jump. There can be a lot of energy in moving 'away from' – I picture it much like a bucking bronco trying to rid itself of the rider. Away from provides lots of energy, and the impetus to change but without a clear direction. Having earlier worked on developing your clear vision, the time is right to harness the energy of the bucking bronco – because now you've got a direction for it – you can harness the energy towards your vision.

In order to raise your game you will need new stimulus: to challenge you, to inspire you and ultimately for you to spot new opportunities. Chapter 10 describes some ways in which you can find this new stimulus, and I introduce four simple approaches to give you new information from every encounter. One example is changing the questions you ask, which is a powerful way to elicit more information.

A common objection to achieving more is not having enough time. Often it's less about your time; it's about how you prioritise. Chapter 11 will take you through a way to prioritise what's important to you.

We return to your vision, after it's had time to prove. Chapter 12 will begin the process of turning your vision into workable plans with goals. Within this chapter is a powerful approach called 'outcome thinking', which will robustly kneed your vision to ensure that it fits with all aspects of your life. Once you've put your vision through the outcome planning process, I'll then describe the benefits of having small, underwhelming goals and daily targets to keep you on track for both when things are going well, and when you face the inevitable dip.

Having now got clearer on your goals, I'll explore two common mistakes people make when presenting themselves. One mistake is "not looking the part" of a successful business person. Whilst we like to think that other people will judge us on our contribution, sadly people do make decisions about working with people based on appearance. Chapter 13 has some practical advice as to how to professionalise your clothing in the same way that you professionalise other aspects of your business. The second aspect is around how you verbally present yourself to others. The aim is that your words are spoken with such clarity that they have you front of mind when opportunities (which are 'right up your street') present themselves.

The final chapter addresses the common mistake that people think they have to set and achieve their goals themselves. This is not true. We all work best with a team of people to bounce ideas off, to provide new sources of stimulation and to hold us accountable. The final chapter explores one small aspect of the role of the coach in keeping you focused on achieving and exceeding your goals.

My wish for you is that you *raise your game,* achieve transformational results which will not only benefit you personally but will
make the world a better place for us all to live.

"To your success!"

CHAPTER ONE

Success - the upside and downside

"Experience is not what happens to a man; it is what a man does with what happens to him."

~ ALDOUS HUXLEY

Setting the scene

You want to raise your game. To have this clarity on the next phase in your life is such a positive starting point – congratulations, you've taken the first step. Often this first step is the most difficult – it involves a decision – but you've taken it, congratulations!

When you've achieved your goals, it's useful to set new ones, and it's also important to take time to acknowledge and celebrate where you are now. In Chapter 4 you'll list some of your core skills, your strengths and capabilities that have led you to the success that you've achieved today. Some of those strengths will continue to be relevant as you further your development and begin the journey to achieve transformational results.

Setting new goals and having an overarching clear and compelling vision that propels you forward and, something that 'drives' you in a positive manner, can be an immense source of energy and motivation.[1] With a clear destination in mind, you can set and refine your goals. Not woolly goals that you're not motivated by, but clear and specific goals. Whilst this book will provide a terrific starting point, I'll encourage you to have an unreasonable friend to keep you accountable – to do what you say you will do – and to support you on your journey to raise your game. Typically I recommend either a business or executive coach – Chapter 14 will explore this further.

Celebrate success

As Brits, we are not great at celebrating our own success, or the success of others. This can mean that we don't acknowledge how far we've come, or recognise that it's time to set new challenges. If you have achieved big goals you will know that sometimes achieving them can be momentarily euphoric and then the moment passes, especially if you "don't want to make a fuss", or if you fear that "pride comes before a fall". Even the focus on the next 'to do' distracts us from celebrating. The next 'to do' may not involve setting new goals and, before you know it, gentle ennui has set in.

Many people sometimes don't celebrate their successes. It means that people discount or minimise what they've achieved and they're not rewarding their effort in having set and achieved goals.

Celebrate both effort and success. Celebrating is a pleasurable experience. We like pleasure – it's been found that given a choice animals prioritise pleasure over food. By not celebrating we're denying ourselves positive emotions – which are good for us (more in Chapter 8). By celebrating effort we're more likely to persevere and 'work at' something in the future.

Not celebrating success does nothing to motivate you for the future. Additionally, you may not consciously realise that you've achieved your goals. Celebrating can give you the opportunity to bask in your glory, and it also highlights you are also ready to set your next challenge.

Celebrating success can be slightly counter cultural, "it's just not what we do around here". This book will encourage you to be an observer of culture, and will challenge you to do things differently – after all you want to raise your game and achieve transformational results, this in itself is counter cultural because not everyone does that.

The downside of success

You have probably achieved loads! Many people don't always realise exactly what they've achieved. They're too busy to notice. The good news is that you can take some time to pause and reflect and to celebrate your past successes. Your past successes can define you as much as the learnings that you got when things didn't go quite according to plan. However, having achieved success can sometimes mean that we can get stuck. With this 'stuckness', boredom slowly starts to encroach on life.

Sometimes this 'nagging' feeling of boredom can be lost in busyness of day-to-day life. What starts out as a small nagging feeling generally grows often into full blown boredom – through to stagnation. Many people don't realise they've plateaued. I suspect you're reading this book because at some level you realise you're ready for your next challenge.

I've coached people who have reached the top of their game, and yet they start to notice a small nagging feeling – dissatisfaction is too strong a term for it – yet it starts as a 'niggle' or something that they pay attention to that tells that despite their success, 'something' they can't quite put their finger on is missing.

If in one domain of their life there is no challenge – sometimes people can often find their challenge, flow or excitement in different places. This can be deliberate or accidental. Perhaps you've found yourself taking on a new project at home, joining a committee, or taking on a new hobby – but that's often just a distraction that masking the underlying problem. You're bored.

If you're not sure if you have plateaued or are stagnating, ask yourself the following questions:

● When was I last out of my depth?

● When was I in a situation that I didn't really know exactly how to handle?

● When did I last meet with people who challenged my thinking?

Is your comfort zone too comfortable?

You may have come across the terms "comfort zone" and "stretch zone" (see figure 1). Growth does not happen from within our comfort zone. Often success breeds comfort.

Comfort, stretch and panic zones

Figure 1 – *Comfort Zone*

Be honest with yourself, and ask yourself: am I comfortable in most situations? What sorts of situations give me a much needed stretch? How often do I enter my stretch zone? Do I know what is a stretch for me? When was the last time my abilities were s-t-r-e-t-c-h-e-d?

Having an appropriate level of challenges gives us an experience that is often described as "being in flow", or in "the zone" (not the comfort zone).[2] This state of flow comes from having an appropriate balance of skills to the level of challenge presented. Of course as your skills increase you're likely to be able to deal with challenges of increasing complexity. When you can deal with challenges 'with your eyes closed' then they are no longer a challenge. Without the challenge, then we don't experience 'flow', and that's where the boredom sets in.

Boredom doesn't just affect you. You know this because at some time in your life you have met someone who is bored (not necessarily boring); you know that their energy can be a drain on you, that at some level they've become listless. Think for a moment of the long-term effects of boredom on health, on relationships – both at home and work – and of course on your enthusiasm for the business that you run.

If you're not enthused and motivated, how likely is it that your team are? Whether you like it or not your team will pick up cues from you. If you think that your team's become a bit listless recently, first take a look at yourself – and you're already taking action to change that.

Where do you find your excitement?

Being in the zone, or in flow, isn't the only place you can find a challenge to the boredom. Much research nowadays points to three main ways a person can find well-being – which is an important step on the way to achieving transformational results.

Ways to challenge boredom

| Enjoy the moment | Be in flow | Finding meaning & purpose |

Figure 2 – *Where do you find challenge?*

Do you live for the moment?

The picture on the left represents living what's sometimes described as the 'high life', a more hedonistic lifestyle: "eat, drink and be merry". These are (the sometimes fleeting) moments of pleasure that pass and often leave us craving the next one. Perhaps you have found that success has allowed you more of those moments, and whilst they are great, for most successful people they're not enough. Of course, these hedonic moments can and most definitely should be enjoyed in relation to the other two. Chapter 8 will shed more light on the importance of positive experiences, and the resultant positive emotions. For many years the benefits of positive emotions have been overlooked. Recent research shows that positive emotions build your resilience and enable you to see more opportunities.

"Today is a gift.
That is why they call it the present."

~ ELEANOR ROOSEVELT

Do you enjoy being in the zone?

The picture in the middle represents flow – the times when we're so absorbed that we lose the sense of time. Flow is found when the challenge matches or slightly exceeds the skills that you have – it's often more often described in the sporting context – of individuals finding flow, for example, through sailing, rock climbing or horse-riding. However, research shows that many of us can also find flow through our work – a moment of total absorption – when we experience the flow, time has a strange quality. Hours can pass in an instant; moments can appear to last far longer than elapsed time, yet both are in the flow.

Do you feel your life has purpose?

The diagram on the right of figure 1 represents a life of purpose. Many people are able to find meaning in their work that propels them on to greater things. If you don't know your life purpose already, Chapters 5 and 6 will start to explore what's important to you, and what gives your life meaning.

Greedy three

Most people don't have elements of all three ways of overcoming boredom. They predominately use just one or two ways.

All three are important to achieve transformational results.

Not only is it important to celebrate and enjoy the good in life, it's important to be constantly learning, developing mastery and experiencing flow. If in addition we can find or create some form of meaning or purpose in our life, then that will provide the motivation and huge amounts of energy to drive us forward. It also increases our resilience to power through the hard times.

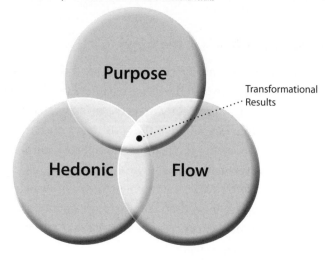

Figure 3 – *Transformational Results*

Take 30 seconds to give yourself a quick assessment. On the diagram above, ask yourself, which have I got? Which are missing? Have they always been missing? What would be a 'quick win' to add more of one that's out of balance?

In *Raise your game* we will address all three of these elements which provide balance and develop resilience: Chapter 8 addresses positive emotions, Chapter 4 addresses activities which have provided you flow, and Chapters 5 and 6 begin to address finding your life purpose.

Have past successes become your security blanket?

Small children often take comfort from a stuffed toy or blanket. I've heard the blanket described as a 'security blanket', and often the child wants it with them. It's a developmental phase that children often go through before they develop into the next stage. Sometimes adults can be less aware of the things that they "hold on to", like the child's security blanket. In this context, it's not likely to be a physical object, although it can be; however, whatever it is, it can prevent you from developing to your next stage.

Ironically success can become a security blanket. We get used to having it. We don't want to leave home without it. However this 'holding on' can cause us at an extreme to stagnate, or hold us back from achieving greater success or happiness since we become fearful of risking losing our current success. However most people have to adapt and evolve to continue their success, otherwise the world will overtake you. The transitional period of: acknowledging success, recognising we want more and, setting a plan in place, allows us to let go of the past. This letting go creates a vacuum, which leaves us open to achieve transformational results in the future.

Success can be a trap – often one which is warm and comfortable at current levels: rewarded well financially, and a 'good enough' lifestyle. For some people they're not easily able to contemplate the perceived risks of doing something different; they can feel overwhelmed to such an extent that they're not able to even think about it. Slowly and insidiously boredom and frustration builds, and that can lead to an erosion in confidence.

Take action.

Before founding my own company, I had a job that I loved. Only a few years earlier it had been my dream job, and as such, I thoroughly enjoyed training and coaching others. I worked for a great company, which was situated in a superb location, along with an enjoyable twenty-mile drive to work. Life was good – and yet – could I do this 'forever'?, and for the next 25+ years until my retirement? I could 'feel' I was ready for my next challenge. I looked around internally for my next challenge – but at the height of the recession – even internal moves were difficult. I was encouraged to 'wait it out' … I could feel the build up of boredom and frustration and knew I needed to do something different.

This book will give you the opportunity to 'take stock' of where you are now and give you some suggestions of what you need to do to achieve transformational results. However, I must give a warning: results will not come from reading (the book) alone. You will have to take action, make choices and change a few things in your life.

I use the term 'taking stock', as one way to look at your life, which is like doing a review of a business. Typically a business has a range of products or services, some yielding high levels of profit, and others lower levels of profit. Some products will be fast moving and others slow moving. Is there a good reason for you to keep the slow moving, low profit items? More importantly, how can you focus more on the activities which give you the highest overall profit? Like the annual stock clear-out, which makes way for new products, you have to be honest with yourself. Find anything (thoughts, beliefs, activities) that's holding you back and be willing to let go. Find what qualities to promote to more prominent space. You can begin to ask yourself: what's working for me now? What worked in the past? What's no longer working? What is it that it is time to let go of?

What I mean is, there may be some activities which you find very energising and yet you're not doing enough of them in your day-to-day activities. Therefore, this process will give you the opportunity to 'design in' more of those activities and to develop – what a friend describes – as a personal business plan. This will be explored further in Chapter 8.

There is also the possibility that there are things that you either for yourself or for the benefit of others, that drain your energy. Consequently there will be times when I encourage you to 'stop it'. I will challenge your beliefs and things you hold dear. My aim is to nudge you outside of your comfort zone. This, almost by definition can be uncomfortable. You can of course choose to stop reading – but I encourage you to keep reading – *and* take some small actions and notice the effect, within these small actions is where growth can be found. Get ready to see more, do more and be more. I have trained and coached thousands of people in these approaches. They work.

What you are about to embark upon is an iterative process. Whilst some people just seem to 'know' what game they're playing, for many of us, finding the bigger game takes some self-discipline, some input from others, and often some feedback too. This often starts as a solo voyage as no one else can define your destination other than you. However, this is not a solo journey; once you set course and declare your destination other people will show up in your life to nudge and support you in your journey. When you're bored, this 'support' can be interpreted as interference. When your course is set, this 'interference' becomes welcome fuel for the journey, propelling you to the next level.

So, you've achieved your goals – what next?

"Our deepest fear is not that we are inadequate.
Our deepest fear is that we are
powerful beyond measure."

~ MARIANNE WILLIAMSON.

You are capable of greatness.

I'm reminded of the story of the traveller who came across a large pig tethered to a small stick in the ground. The pig was easily capable of tearing the stick from the ground – and yet it doesn't. When the traveller asked why the pig had not simply ripped the stick from the ground, the owner simply stated that the pig had been tethered to the stick from being a piglet. As a piglet, the pig did not have the strength to pull out the stick. Over time, the piglet had 'learned' that there was no point in even trying. What was once true, was no longer – but the pig had become trapped by its conditioning.

Perhaps there are things that you learnt previously that are no longer true. Perhaps, there are some conclusions you've reached about life that you can begin to question, which in turn might release you to a whole new level.

> One of my former colleagues was a keen mountain biker, and went on a mountain biking course-cum-holiday. Early in the programme the instructor suggested he raise his saddle so that his legs could be straighter on the pedals, thus giving increased power. As soon as the question: "But don't your feet have to touch the floor?" left my colleagues mouth, he'd realised that the ability to put one's feet on the floor might be a wise recommendation for a five-year-old or a novice, and that wisdom no longer held true for him: the experienced mountain biker that he had become.

Wait for the green man before crossing the road

There are some things that we're told as children that naturally evolve. For example, "always hold mummy's hand when crossing the road" morphs into you being compelled to use the green cross code every time you cross. Most of you can now cross the road without referring to Tufty and I'm guessing that you don't still believe that you *have* to "hold hands with a grown up" whilst crossing the road – that's purely optional.

This road crossing example shows how some things we're told, which are the basis of our beliefs, naturally evolve. However, some things we're told as kids get lodged in our thinking and we become a bit stuck, and they become limitations – you might have heard the expression 'limiting beliefs' – and this is what they are. They're things that we've held to be true, and generally we've never had cause to question them.

Over the following chapters I'm going to present you with ideas and techniques that you can use to challenge yourself in order to raise your awareness. You can then start the process of questioning what you hold to be true, to see if it is fact or an outdated belief. Sometimes limiting beliefs can be spotted by someone else; however, I encourage you to develop your own awareness so that you can increasingly do this for yourself. Finding what has limited you will have a positive impact on your motivation to change. You can also work on the broader aspects of your environment, the places you go and the people that you mix with. You will increase the likelihood of finding people and situations that challenge your thinking, and thus challenging your beliefs and giving yourself new opportunities to grow.

The fallacy of keeping your options open

Most of us are naturally inclined to keep our options open. I think this is human nature. I've reached the conclusion, through experience and observation that you have to overcome this natural instinct in order to achieve transformational results.

Overcoming instinct

Please don't tell me it's not 'right' to overcome instinct. Toddlers are taught how to use a potty – that behaviour doesn't come naturally at first – but very quickly we become socialised to a view of 'natural' that is using the bathroom rather than the street as a latrine.

Keeping options open is not productive

Options are decisions that you haven't yet committed to. We live in a time of many choices and options, and decision making takes energy, no matter the size of the decision. Constantly revisiting decisions is unproductive; it drains energy. Instead raise your game by taking decisions.

Dan Ariely, a behavioural psychologist, demonstrated the 'cost' of indecision by conducting research.[3] His team developed a computer program that showed three different coloured doors. Within the program, by clicking on a door participants in the experiment could enter a room of the same colour. Once in a room each click of the mouse would earn a small amount of money (between one cent and ten cents), and each room had a different earning range. For example, the red room might range from 2–4 cents per click, whilst the blue room had monetary amounts between 4–6 cents, and the green room, 5–7 cents. The objective was to get the most money, which involved finding the room with the biggest payoff and clicking on it as many times as possible. The computer kept a running tally of the amount. In the initial experiment – participants just had to find the room with the biggest pay out and click in the room for the duration of the experiment (100 clicks) to earn the most points.

A devious twist happened in a follow up experiment. Any door left unvisited for twelve clicks would disappear. There was a visual indicator showing how close to disappearing each door was. In this experiment participants were in a frenzy to keep the doors open – clicking between the rooms to stop the doors disappearing – no matter what the payout. Results showed participants instinctively kept their doors (or options) open and typically made 15% less money than those in the first experiment. Ariely suggests: *"The truth is that they could have made more money by picking a room – any room – and merely staying there for the whole experiment!"*

Ask yourself: which options am I keeping open rather than directly focusing my energy on? What does that mean for me in terms of my life or entrepreneurial path? Which options am I keeping open (intentionally or otherwise), which dissipate my energy?

Examine, choose, focus, act, move on!

Ariely also tells a story of a donkey, standing looking at a barn. At each end of the barn is a bale of hay. The donkey, undecided as to which will be the best option, sadly starves whilst looking from one bale of hay to the other. Of course, I'm not suggesting that you'll starve, by keeping your options open, although the reality of the story is not far away.

> I remember meeting a friend in Covent Garden. We had decided on which restaurant prior to meeting and on arrival we were told there would be a wait of up to 30 minutes. Being very hungry and with plenty of other restaurants in close vicinity, I suggested to my friend that we find another restaurant (thinking that they'd be able to seat us immediately). Yup, you guessed it – we wandered around to no avail. That evening Covent Garden seemed very popular, with seemingly no-where able to seat us instantly. Finally, we ended up in a cheap, brightly lit pizza parlour lacking ambiance, having waited far longer to be served food than if we'd committed to the original decision, and accepted the original 30-minute wait.

What often happens is that we don't commit to a course of action because we think there's a better decision to be made. Often this is not the case and our energy has been used up in non-decision.

Choosing a specific destination or having a clear vision can seem counter intuitive to many people, especially when society seems to demand that we be 'open' to possibilities, and to 'roll with it'. However, it is a focused approach that I'll be encouraging you to have as part of this book. You have a particular set of skills, experiences and interests. You have them in a unique combination. With this – what do you want to do? I heard the expression *"doing the best at what you do best"*, which I think is a lovely way of defining success. Where openness *does fit in*, is to keep an open mind – more about that in Chapter 3.

For some people "keep your options open" was something that was repeated at school, by figures in authority whether parents or teachers. Most of us accepted this advice, and now tell ourselves that having open options is more important than a clear and compelling personal vision. I don't agree; Chapter 5 describes more about the importance of vision, which although may close some doors – other doors open which are more aligned to your vision. However doing things differently, perhaps closing doors, involves making changes. For many people the process of change is not as smooth as it can sound, so next I'll describe more about what can happen as you start to make changes in your life.

CHAPTER TWO

The cycle of change

"A man's mind stretched by a new idea can never go back to its original dimensions."

~ OLIVER WENDELL HOLMES, JR.

The antidote to getting stuck, disconnected and ultimately depressed is to initiate some form of change, i.e. you will be doing something differently. This can *sound* easy, often there is something that stops us making and maintaining these changes. This chapter is about the different stages of change that you will experience so that you can be prepared for the ups and downs and ensure you have appropriate support for the journey.

Seeds have a set of ideal environmental conditions in which they germinate. Similarly there are 'ideal' conditions that bring about lasting change.

For lasting change we need to be dissatisfied with our current state of being. This could be general malaise, boredom, or a state of depression. Often what's needed is an internal decision – your voice inside says something like: "Right, something's gotta change!" or "I have had enough of ..." This can provide energy to do *something*, although the "what to do" is not yet defined.

The next step is to have or develop a compelling vision, or life purpose. In the following chapters I'm going to give you a way to connect to your passion. To find the meaning in your life that drives you forward, that re-energises you and provides you with motivation.

Once you know where you are going, it's useful to have the initial steps of your change journey marked out. I don't think it's important to have it all clearly plotted – some of it will evolve, just like a real journey. Driving a car on a dark night, even with headlights you can't see the whole road, never mind the whole route. The headlights show sufficient road to be able to make decisions about the conditions, the important turnings.

 Many people think they should have everything mapped out in a high level of detail.

 Significant markers and milestones work just fine.

 Conversely it is a mistake to have nothing mapped out, no destination, waiting to see "what will come up".

 Know where you're heading. Even hitchhikers have a vague destination in mind.

Warning

There are implications to making changes. The change journey is not an easy path; it leads to being in control of one's life, and with control means decisions and occasionally regret for choices you have taken. Doing nothing can seem like the attractive option, and it can also be like a time lapse series of photographs of a bowl of fruit – just waiting for the inevitable rot and decay. In a subtle way not taking action becomes a decision. Inactivity in a moving world will cause you to regress.

In the short term there will be activities for you to do, some self- reflection and developing insights about your strengths, although I'm not suggesting protracted periods of naval gazing. However, it is useful to build on your already strong foundations – so the reflection is just about checking you know what forms your foundations, to make any minor adjustments that you wish to prior to building your future. Or going through this process you may decide it is time for a larger life change, either way, you will be able to correctly assess which course of action and be empowered to take it.

I will challenge you to create some big hairy audacious goals for yourself.[4] These goals are important because you may feel some fear around changing things that are seemingly working 'FINE'. Especially when your life is already comfortable – there will be times when you ask yourself: "Why am I bothering?" This is a natural response. However, in order to create transformation results for yourself you will have to overcome these natural responses.

Although you've put in the effort and changed in the past, I'm not sure that it's easier the second time around. I think one of the reasons it's not easier is that your starting point is one of relative comfort, whereas the first time you achieved success you probably came from 'nothing' and had less to lose. Furthermore, the feelings associated with change can be disquieting. These feelings can be very different from feelings of 'comfort' you've become used to.

Our memory can play tricks on us, and we often forget the effort involved. Do you remember learning a new skill? Perhaps learning to drive, there's a stage when you know what to do – and yet the movements just don't seem natural. Pushing through this phase takes discipline, commitment and perseverance.

Let me say this in a slightly different way to emphasise the point. All change in the middle looks (and feels) like failure. I think it's important for you to know this – so that from this vantage point of comfort and safety, **before** setting on your journey you can actively weigh up the advantages and disadvantages of change, and should you decide to 'go for it', then you can also design your strategies to support you through the sticky and uncomfortable middle bits.

Seth Godin wrote an excellent book: *The Dip*, which eloquently describes a 'dip' that accompanies change.[5] In the dip there will be times when you are reluctant to put in the effort, times when it just all seems too much like hard work. There's the expression, "the night is darkest in the hour before dawn". It's useful to know that dawn is beyond the darkest hour, and Godin describes what you can do when you find yourself in the dip – and you will. Some writers on change seem to suggest that the dip has to be significant for change to take root, for it to become permanent, although it's been found that events don't have to be traumatic to have permanent beneficial shift.[6]

Take a moment to reflect, ask yourself:

- What examples do I have in my life of where I continued with a course of action, even when I didn't feel like it, or it seemed that the situation was conspiring against me?

- How does having these examples change or support my decision to embark on transformational results?

All work involves elements of repetition – what do you want to repeat?

I realised relatively early in my career that all work involved an element of repetition; certainly to get good at something we need to do it time and time again. Providing we're getting useful feedback and making the appropriate changes, it's likely that over time we get better and better at the things that we repeat.

It is a mistake to believe that just because you repeat something, you will be getting better at it. Not all repetition leads to improvement. Mindless repetition leads to the 'same old' results.

Repetition, with tweaks, modifications and adaptions combined with feedback and awareness is what leads to improvements.

Mistakes

Mistakes do happen. Sadly much in society seems to teach us to be ashamed of our mistakes. Quite often, the school system trains us that the only answer is the 'right' answer, and that there *is* such a thing as a right answer, and of course life's not like that.

It is a mistake not wanting to make mistakes. This restricts learning. You might mistakenly believe that making mistakes means that what you're trying doesn't 'come naturally', and therefore should be abandoned.

Revel in learning from your mistakes

It is too easy to become ashamed by mistakes, which leads us to reach the (often sub-conscious) conclusion: "I'm not putting myself in that type of situation again", and in that instant we become closed to learning. This 'conclusion' on one hand protects us from being ashamed, and can prevent us from learning anything new (because we don't allow themselves to be in that position). More on this in the next chapter when I describe mindsets.

Big clangers and small 'bloopers'

Big clangers or big mistakes, and hopefully the associated learning stays with us for years. However often the small mistakes get forgotten. Whilst this is convenient – because otherwise we may never try anything new – it also means that when we don't experience immediate results we can become quickly disillusioned, forgetting the time, effort and mistakes we've made in the past in learning other skills. Thus it becomes too easy to dismiss learning new skills because 'it doesn't come naturally'.

The benefits of being a slow learner

It is the expectation that new skills can be learned 'overnight'. Many people don't know how learning takes place. I've noticed that when learning a new skill, people become quickly disillusioned, almost expecting to transition from unskilled to super mastery to happen overnight if not sooner.

Know how you learn, and be gentle with yourself if you don't pick something up instantly.

When overnight transformation doesn't happen, people 'rubbish' the skill that they're trying to learn, saying it's not useful or necessary. Perhaps, because in some areas of life I'm a slow (but persistent) learner, I've become painfully acquainted with each step in the learning process. For example, now I would describe myself as a reasonably competent skier – and I also know that it took weeks (and at one week a year – literally years) to learn how to ski.

Perhaps you have found yourself frustrated with the slowness of your learning, and have quickly decided that whatever you're practicing "is not for you", "you're not a natural", and therefore you quit. This frustration and lack of determination and persistence to overcome can be a barrier to change. Achieving transformational results will involve you doing something different, at least in the short term. This 'doing different' is likely to involve some form of learning, either in the activities that you do or the way you think about things. It's likely to be accompanied by a dip – know that it's likely to happen and have plans in place to keep pushing through it!

What are the stages of learning?

There are different models of learning. The approach I'm going to use is the *unconscious competence* model, which is typically used when learning a new skill. Whilst the names of the stages are slightly insulting (who likes to be called incompetent?), the advantage is that it shows that learning is a process rather than instantaneous.

Four Stages of Learning

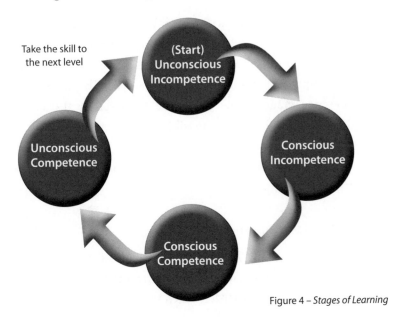

Take the skill to the next level

(Start) Unconscious Incompetence

Conscious Incompetence

Conscious Competence

Unconscious Competence

Figure 4 – *Stages of Learning*

Often in hindsight I believe we forget the effort involved in learning and change. Sure, some things are easier for some people than others – perhaps you are a natural sports person but what about financials or languages? It is a rare individual who is equally adept across a range of disciplines. There's a strong likelihood that you have persevered in at least one area to learn something new – and it's this perseverance I want you to remember, rediscover and harness to your advantage going forward.

> Surely one minute I was thinking about learning to drive a car – and the next moment – I was a competent driver … Hmmm, I had forgotten the 30 hours of lessons, plus my dad taking me out for two days of driving to develop my 'road awareness' the weekend before my test.

Unconscious Incompetence

The first stage in the learning process is unconscious incompetence – learning to drive a car is an example that most people can relate to. At the most pure, it's a child who jumps in the car with learning to drive simply not being on their radar yet. The unconscious incompetence stage is the naïve me who sat in the car and thought: "How hard can this possibly be … even my granny does it." (At 17, I thought I knew more than granny!). When learning any skill, this stage of naïve bliss is quickly followed by the stage of conscious incompetence.

Conscious Incompetence

The stage of conscious incompetence, involved me kangarooing down the road struggling with clutch control and the sudden jolt of realisation that driving is harder than it looks. In learning terms, this is where people start to realise that the new skill is a bit harder than it first seems. Often, we become aware of our own incompetence, which can be a brutal awaking.

Many people find their emotions at this stage overwhelming, and they 'give up' learning or persevering – i.e. they quit, exactly when they are developing new skills.

Knowing in advance that this stage will happen – plan ahead to how you will support yourself through this frustrating time.

Conscious Competence

Of course slowly but surely I began to drive with full concerted concentration. This skill of driving is putting together many smaller skills. Every time I was getting to grips with one skill e.g. reversing in a straight line, another one was quickly added – reversing round a corner or the three-point turn. I was jumping through these first three stages for each new skill. Eventually I achieved conscious competence for all of the skills, and with concentration had the skills to pass the driving test.

Unconscious Competence

Around that time I remember meeting up with one of my friends, who had passed her driving test. She drove with one hand on the steering wheel, cigarette in the other, and she had the radio blaring. I remember admiring her seeming competence at being able to 'do all those things at once'. I'm not advocating smoking, or driving single handed whilst distracted by the radio, the point I am making is about when the skill comes together it seems 'natural' and there's a tendency to take it for granted. When the skill has been well learnt to the extent that it's automatic, in learning terms the phrase that's often used is unconscious competence.

Building advanced skills

Of course taking your skills to an advanced level will take you back to the beginning of the model and unconscious incompetence – or specifically to a probable lack of competence in 'advanced' driving skills. As can be seen from the above example although driving single handed seems 'natural', it doesn't necessarily follow that this is an 'expert' level of skill. To become an Advanced Driver, or to become a rally driver some skills would have to be unlearned, which takes the learner quickly from a state of unconscious (in)competence though to conscious incompetence.

Different support at different stages

The first step is knowing that there are different stages to learning and change, and you'll quickly realise that as you go through the stages you'll need different support at different times. Sometimes you'll need direct 'how to' instructions; other times, you'll need feedback about what's working and what needs attention so that you can make changes. At other times, when you're feeling frustrated that it doesn't yet feel that it's 'coming together', this is when emotional support and encouragement to continue is what's needed. Knowing in advance that there are different stages means that you can put the support in place. Perhaps you intuitively know who to speak to at different times. Chapter 14 looks at the different types of support, and encourages you to think who will be the best person to support you in your journey to raising your game and achieving transformational results.

CHAPTER THREE

Develop a growth mindset

"Whether you think you can or whether you think you can't you're right."

~ HENRY FORD

You've been successful, you have the right attitude. Right? Possibly.

Successful people can become stuck in their ways and patterns of thinking.

Explore different ways of thinking about things.

Think about it for a moment. The things that have led to success become *the* way of doing things. Success literally gets engraved on the brain. Neural networks are created, and these thinking patterns are re-enforced.[7] And yet, the external environment changes, technology and economic conditions change, even the political landscape changes – are you sure you're adapting to the new conditions? There's an expression: "If it's not growing, it's dying." Ask yourself: How much am I growing?

This chapter is about how you can adopt a mindset of growth and begin to prime your mindset for your next phase of success to achieve transformational results.

I use the expression: **Mindset X Activities = Results**

Often we're clear on some of the results we want (the things we want to 'have' and 'give'). Many of us realise that some activity (things we need to 'do') will be required in order to get those results. However Dweck has shown that something called mindset has a huge impact on results.[8]

I believe mindset and activities work together in a similar way to a mathematical formula:

1X1=1	*Equal input of mindset and action gives modest results.*
1X13=13	*Results increase commensurate with the increase in activity.*
2X13=26	*A small shift in mindset has the effect of doubling results.*
0X13=0	*Despite activity, notice what happens when the mindset is not right.*
0X26=0	*Even frantic activity – doesn't translate into results without the appropriate mindset.*

 Many people don't spend enough time working on their mindset.

 Develop a growth mindset.

Activity is good; indeed, it's essential. However, it's useful also to focus your attention on your 'be' or mindset, which can be the multiplier in achieving transformational results.

Often the concept of 'attitude' has been a woolly term, hard to pin down what it means when someone has the 'right attitude'. Recent research from academic researcher Carole Dweck from the field of psychology, supports the fact that there are indeed different attitudes or mindsets, and that these differences have a marked effect on results.

Dweck essentially describes two different mindsets: the growth mindset and the fixed mindset.

The fixed mindset

The fixed mindset is where a person's beliefs about themselves and others are fixed and unchangeable. Think about your views of intelligence. Do you believe intelligence is a fixed trait that can't be changed, or perhaps that it's a more malleable part of a person's make-up?

When a person holds a fixed mindset about an aspect of themselves or another person, they believe that traits such as intelligence are fixed and can't be changed. Often it means that they don't willingly engage in the new activity, they don't pursue learning, and therefore their results become self-fulfilling: they get what they expect! They don't believe they can do something, and without effort, experiencing the odd failure and learning from it ... guess what – they don't learn to do something different.

It's probably a useful aside to mention that the *person* isn't 'fixed', it's merely an 'attitude' that becomes fixed. This attitude is held about a particular area of one's life – and of course attitudes can and do change – don't take my word for it - there's research supporting that this change can and does happen.[9]

In my observations, I've noticed that sometimes success can cause people to fix their mindset and stagnate. I wonder if achieving success causes people to become slightly entrenched and less open to new information because they think "this way worked once, it should work again". It's only by setting new, higher goals that the change process can really begin. When our responses become too automatic it closes down our ability to see new opportunities.

Stimulus, response

You may have heard of Mr Pavlov and his dogs. He trained his dogs to salivate at the sound of a bell, which the dogs came to associate with receiving food. However, we are more than organisms that respond to stimulus. Sometimes people do become entrenched in patterns of behaving that are predictable, and on the whole, that's fine. For example, the morning alarm sounds (stimulus), and we get out of bed (response). When someone asks us a question (stimulus), and we know the answer, we respond. However, we are more than this automatic response. We have choice in how we respond.

 Many people forget they have a choice and think the other person 'caused' them to behave in a certain way. They behave like Pavlov's dogs when they are far more capable.

 In order to recover this choice, my top tip is to take a breath. That's often all it takes to consider whether the way you've always responded is actually the most effective, and whether there might be useful alternative ways to respond.

The topic of choice is a meaty one – and one that's very important. In some areas of our life it's useful to automate our choices so we don't spend unnecessary time and mental energy deliberating minor decisions. Chapter 9 has more information on choices. For now, suffice it to say that making a decision does mean closing a door. Saying 'yes' to one thing often means saying 'no' to something else. By consistently not making decisions and choices, progress is delayed. Become a master of decision making, take action, make progress and achieve great things.

The growth mindset

The growth mindset has been shown to be more effective in producing higher results. With the growth mindset comes a willingness to learn. With a growth mindset, effort, persistence and dedication, you can change almost every aspect of yourself – if you so wish.

Ask yourself:

- When was the last time I tried something new?
- When was the last time I was outside of my comfort zone?

Dweck's research has shown that even children as young as four have started to develop either a fixed or growth mindset. They offered children the choice of redoing an easy jigsaw puzzle or they could try a harder one. The children with the fixed mindset played it safe, not risking mistakes, whereas children with the growth mindset thought that was a strange choice to be offered to do the same puzzle again, taking delight in the new challenge. Children with the fixed mindset want to succeed, but children with the growth mindset, success is about stretching themselves.

Different mindsets in different areas of your life

Neither the fixed nor the growth mindset is right or wrong. However, transformational results are more likely to occur in areas where a growth mindset is adopted because you're more likely to do new things – to learn from them – and see new opportunities.

You have different mindsets in different areas of your life. As you think about the skills in any of the following areas, for example, juggling, playing golf, singing, business, sales administration, there are probably areas that you are open to learning. "Sure, I'll take some advice on how to improve my golf swing in order to improve my handicap." Whereas, there will be other areas where a fixed mindset will kick in: "Sing? Me? Never!" It's useful to be aware of a situation where you use a growth mindset and fixed mindset, and the next section will give you some pointers to spot each, and then how to change into the growth mindset at will.

Which mindset are you using?

I mentioned earlier that some effort will be required on your part. Become alert to which mindset is operating in which environment. You can start to notice the attributes of both, so that ultimately you can adjust to the growth mindset, and be open to new learning and new opportunities in any situation.

The awareness that's required to notice your mindset moment by moment is quite hard ... so my initial recommendation would be to take five minutes towards the end of your work day. Think of the day that's taken place, and the evening before. Jot down the key activities that you were involved with and take a moment to remember whether they caused you to become a bit closed and defensive (signs of the fixed mindset), or whether you were open, curious and questioning (indicators of the growth mindset). More indicators follow.

Noticing the fixed mindset

If you notice yourself responding with "yeah, yeah, I know", you're closing down to new information, or perhaps in hindsight you noticed that something had caused you to become defensive – these are pretty good indicators of a fixed mindset.

Ask yourself: when I get into a fixed mindset, how do I feel? What thoughts run through my mind? What's my posture like? What words or phrases do I regularly hear myself say? What do I think about change? What am I slightly fearful about? How do I feel about my success? Do I fear losing it?

I'm not equating a fixed mindset to depression, but I think our posture is important in changing how we feel — and we can change our posture. In one *Charlie Brown* comic-strip, *Charlie Brown* is demonstrating his 'depressed stance' to Lucy. He's standing with his head bent towards the ground and shoulders slumped. He explains: "When you're depressed, it makes a lot of difference how you stand. The worst thing you can do is straighten up and hold your head high because then you'll start to feel better," he says as he stands erect, shoulders squared and his head held high.

Noticing the growth mindset

You've probably got more of a growth mindset in situations where you notice that you're curious for more information, where you ask questions. You may also notice yourself making the odd mistake, and depending on the context you might find you can gently laugh at yourself, and delight in finding new information.

When you notice that you're in a more growth mindset, how do you feel? What thoughts run through your mind? What's your posture like? What words or phrases do you regularly hear yourself say, either to yourself and others?

So what?

Notice:

- That you have both the fixed and growth mindset.
- That you use both in different circumstances.
- That the growth and fixed mindset cause you to behave differently.

It would be great to have had the insight that the growth mindset is more effective for growth, and that growth is what's needed to achieve transformational results.

Noticing which mindset was employed in any situation in hindsight is the first step.

Advanced mindset skills

The advanced training is being able to spot which mindset you're using moment by moment, **and also** to have the ability to switch into the growth mindset as easily and simply as you switch on your kettle. One phrase that can be a handy switching mechanism is to say to yourself "mmmm, that's interesting" (which effectively breaks the automatic stimulus response pattern), take a breath, ask yourself a question, and change your body posture to keep an open mind.

The benefits of a growth mindset

"The real voyage of discovery consists not in seeking new landscapes but in having new eyes."

~ MARCEL PROUST

With your already demonstrated success, having an open mindset ensures you're alert to new opportunities. Opportunities are available to us all – so why is it that sometimes only relatively few people see them. Some people just see the world differently, and maintaining a growth mindset is one way that you can see the world differently. When you look at a situation you can ask yourself, and others: what's new about this situation? What can I learn from it? Where's the opportunity? This is very different from a more closed, fixed mindset response of: "I've seen this before; just like the last one."

A growth mindset also means you're more likely to persevere through both the frustrations and excitement of learning. In the depth of that frustration, it's even more important to have the ability to maintain the growth mindset – or switch into it as soon as you notice language of self-doubt creeping in: "I can't do this, it's too hard; I should never have started this ..."

Whilst change can happen through altering your mindset and creating a compelling vision, significant and transformational change is likely to come through a large number of deliberate small changes, whereby you can actively make change and monitor the response. You have to have a growth mindset to get the most from these activities. More on this in Chapter 7.

Mindset is the first step to look at to ensure you're open to new opportunities and ready to commence this journey to transformational results. Let's first acknowledge that you are an experienced traveller, you probably know the type of things to pack and you're worldly wise. Remember the destination is new – so it's handy to remember to keep an open mind to navigate past the obstacles and to find opportunities, which are sometimes nestling in obscure corners.

One of the quickest ways to change your mindset is to change some of the environmental factors, the people you hang out with, and the books you read. This is covered in more detail in Chapter 10. One of my mentors described it this way: *"Good books and good company stop the weeds from growing in your mind."*

Are you ready for warp speed?

Changing your mindset sounds quite a small thing to do, although it's highly likely that you will experience knock-on effects, and some of them you may not experience as 'nice' – certainly initially! For example: you're more likely to get stuck more often as you try new things. You'll experience what feels like 'failure'. You'll notice when others have a fixed mindset, and you might find you want to evangelise over growth mindsets. You'll be the one asking questions rather than having all the answers – which at first can be frustrating. However, persevere – it's worth it in the end!

During this time it's useful to stay connected with your vision. Your ultimate goal is that you achieve transformational results. Transformational change will have a positive knock-on effect on your current situation, for example: your family, your partner, your children, your friends. Although you can't double guess the impact of the transformational results, it's useful to acknowledge that your life will change. You will literally become a new person – as you think about change and transformational results – are you ready?

One approach to help you think through the implications is outcome thinking, which is covered extensively in Chapter 12. First, let's get you clearer on the direction for warp speed, by first discovering your strengths, successes, and finding your success themes.

CHAPTER FOUR

Appraise your assets

"We are what we repeatedly do.
Excellence, then, is not an act, but a habit."
~ ARISTOTLE

Before you look forward and develop your vision, it's useful to take a backward glance at your past. This looking back is not in some 'deep' way. It's useful to understand your past, as this provides the foundations for building your future.

Mining your past for value

Reflect on your successes, mine them for the value that they contain. This can provide rich information as to what type of situations bring out the best in you, and have already inspired you to greatness. I'll be encouraging you to think about what it was about you, or perhaps the situation that seemed to lead to that success. It will also encourage and remind you that you have achieved success before and have come through challenges, and that you can do it again! And again, especially with the growth mindset.

Celebrate your past successes

As I described in Chapter 1, it can be incredibly powerful to take some time to acknowledge and celebrate your achievements. Often when we're on the fast paced journey, continually striving for the next achievement we rarely look back to where we started, and acknowledge just how far we've come, and the successes we've had. Take time to celebrate, savour achievements – it provides much needed fuel for facing the next challenge.

What have been your successes?

What is important is recognising the successes, learning how you were successful is as important as the success itself. Take at least 20 minutes to complete this activity.

1. **On an A4 piece of paper, list your successes.**
   Successes are the things you're proud of, both big and small. They could be significant jobs you've done or specific events or situations that you're most proud of, or it could be something that only you know about or even learning a new skill. Your successes do not have to be business related.

   Ask yourself: what gets me fired up in the morning? Is there a particular element of my business or personal life which I think "yeah"! In what situations have I been the most productive?

2. **For each success, consider:**
   - What you're most proud of about it.
   - What you enjoyed, and what led you to it.
   - Think about the state of flow described in Chapter 1, which successes were easy and natural – a good balance between challenge and skill, and which were harder fought?

3. **Look for the patterns and themes that link your successes.**
   Spotting themes is information often only available in hindsight. Think of a child threading beads. At the time the beads go on to the thread, they seem to be random; in hindsight it's much easier to discern a pattern. It's often the

same with business, whilst some jumps and success are planned; usually it's only with the benefit of hindsight that connecting themes and patterns can be seen in what links them together.

Steve Jobs, co-founder of *Apple Computers* and *Pixar Animations* in his 2005 Stanford Commencement Address, eloquently described this by saying "You can't connect the dots looking forwards; you can only connect them looking backward." He described his time at university and dropping in on a calligraphy course, which at the time seemed to have no benefit. It was only ten years later when designing the Mac computer that this understanding of beautiful lettering and spacing became apparent. Take a look at Steve Jobs' 2005 Stanford Commencement Address, on YouTube:

http://www.youtube.com/watch?v=UF8uR6Z6KLc

Perhaps you made some deliberate choices around what you're good at, or around what you enjoyed (possibly they're the same). Were there factors you disliked that led you away from certain situations and by chance into something new? These could have been around people, the culture or the environment.

There are no right or wrong answers, and no one else will see this. It's for you to find what might link, which often gives incredible insight as to the direction in which you might find your next success.

- What is similar between successes?
- What is different?
- If someone else were to look, then what would they think was the theme?
- As you look at the successes, what's the lasting emotion?
- What connects your successes together, and what's the pattern that you can see?

Past successes are a rich seam of information about what drives you, and what you're passionate about. It's an opportunity to recognise some of the elements that have been important to you. This information can provide a useful springboard from which to launch yourself.

Strengths

Mistake *Many people don't know what their strengths are.*

TIP **Find your strengths and ways to use them more frequently**

Just doing something well does not mean it's a 'true strength'. I believe for something to be a 'true strength' you have to enjoy it too. Sometimes we get good at a range of activities that we don't really enjoy, and some people have become good at things that they think they 'ought' to do, or 'should' do. If you want to raise your game it's useful to consider what you do well, as well as what you enjoy, because when you enjoy something you're also likely to spend more time engaged in it, and you'll be energised by it. Additionally, doing things that you enjoy often creates a state of flow, and builds positive emotions. Essentially, positive emotions build resilience and enable you to see more opportunities. The importance of positive emotions will be covered in more detail in Chapter 8.

Finding and knowing your full range of strengths develops your awareness of what your true strengths are. In addition, it can provide a strong foundation for understanding any potential strengths gaps, which you can begin to fill. Understanding your strengths means that you can find the things that you're naturally good at. When you find things you're not naturally good at – or dislike – hire someone to do those tasks.

Sometimes we overlook what comes easily to us – this is a moment to reflect on those things! We live in a culture where often the focus is on addressing weaknesses, and often people develop considerable skills in their weaker areas. Strengths is a great way to think about activities in your life that you're good at **and** that you enjoy, and therefore are intrinsically motivating.

How do you find your strengths

There are different ways you can find out about your strengths:

- Reflect; you will know some of them already.
- You can ask others – either formally or informally.
- The VIA Institute provides a free on-line survey http://www.viacharacter.org/SURVEYS.aspx
- Realise 2 provide a relatively inexpensive standard questionnaire http://www.cappeu.com/Realise2.aspx
- Strengths finder, which is based on research by Gallup http://www.strengthsfinder.com

There are several psychometric tools which can provide you with insights about your natural style, which can provide insight into your strengths. For example, the Myers Briggs Type Indicator (MBTI) can provide a useful starting point, as can DISC. A qualified coach can take you through these tools.

Once you have found your strengths you can really start to notice where and when you use them, and you can also start to find new ways to use your strengths. For example, if you're naturally outgoing and, enjoy talking with people, you might find that you enjoy attending networking events. You may get more insights into the tasks that you really don't enjoy – it's useful to recognise that others will love the jobs you hate. Delegating and outsourcing are covered more fully in Chapter 11.

HOWEVER, these tools and your strengths are just the starting point. Strengths can be a double edged sword.

 Many people assume that their strengths are fixed and unchangeable, which starts to 'fix' the mindset.

 Be open to the different skills that you use, and the different qualities that you have can help to ensure that you remain open and growing.

 Strengths sometimes become overused, at which point they risk becoming a weakness.

One client described himself as "good with people"; however, his strength came at the expense of a focus on business results, because he was too busy focusing on building a solid relationship.

I do use strengths tools, as they do point to what you do well, and can be a great starting point. However, as a human being your job is to develop – to develop beyond any limitation imposed by psychometric tools, however good they may be.

Do you have room in your life for your next successes?

It's great to have trophies, certificates and mementoes such as photos from our past successes – **and** please ensure that you have space for the new ones! "Nature abhors a vacuum", so ensure that you have space for your future successes.

Successes are great; however, people often feel that they learn more when things didn't go 'to plan.'

When things didn't go to plan

"I have not failed. I've just found 10,000 ways that won't work."

~ **THOMAS EDISON ON INVENTING THE LIGHT BULB.**

We all make mistakes. Making mistakes is an opportunity to learn; in fact, if you don't learn, it's likely you'll develop more of a fixed mindset and risk the longer-term consequences of stagnating. When we learn "what hasn't worked", we have the opportunity to do something different.

Some people fear making mistakes, or get hung up on mistakes from their past and therefore fear repeating mistakes. It's therefore important to make a note of what you learnt.

ACTIVITY   What did you learn from situations when things didn't go to plan?

If you find yourself stuck replaying a situation from the past

You might have intense feelings about a past event; these feelings don't change anything about the situation and can hold you back.

If the feelings are intense and on regular replay, it's likely that your brain's processing power is taken with continual re-processing of the event and your emotions. If you want to achieve transformational results it's time to draw a line under the situation and focus your energies on future successes. You may choose to enlist the support of a professional – more on this later, first I'll explore what it's costing you in terms of your mental processing power.

Clearing your prime thinking space

Your thinking space is, to coin an American expression, like "prime real estate". You want to ensure that you're getting the highest value from it in rents. Negative thoughts about the past are like squatters on your real estate. They're not adding any value, and are preventing you from making money.

There are different types of thoughts that you might find squatting in your thinking space. You might be able to notice whether these thoughts are typically past or future focused?

Many people worry about the future. People cycle through alternative scenarios thinking about 'what if', they have concerns, worries and fears about the future. One antidote is to be clear on your concerns and to take appropriate actions.

For past events, events that have already happened, emotions from the past creep in: regret, guilt, and disappointment. I'll next explore how you can handle ruminating thoughts over past events.

Drawing a line under the event

If something has happened in the past and you find yourself ruminating over it, is there something that you could do that changes the effects of what happened? If there *is* something you can do, take thoughtful action. The action may simply be to write what you learned from the situation, so that you know that you have a record of it, and can move on. Your brain can then stop mulling it over. Squatters evicted! Your prime mental processing power is now free to focus on achieving transformational results.

If that's not enough …

Sometimes these negative and recurring thoughts can be deep rooted. With the appropriate tools and, if you're willing to do the work, they can be relatively quickly snipped out. Sometimes it's useful to call in the services of a professional to assist in this area.

Take an analogy of having a beautiful tree in your garden. A large branch has become diseased and if the branch were heavy and perhaps in an awkward area, you might call in a tree surgeon to safely remove the heavy branch, to preserve both the beauty and health of the tree. In the same way you might call in a specialist to deal with changing the intensity of your emotions around past events. Of course they can't change the event, but they can usually change your feelings about the situation, which should be enough to get your mental processing back on track and ready to achieve transformational results.

Choosing your specialist

Not all therapists / counsellors / coaches can do this speed work, or work at this depth. Therefore, you will need to be clear on what you want, and check with them that they work with short-term clients in the area of interest to you. Ensure you spend some time talking to them before you agree to purchase their services. It can be useful to ensure that you have a good rapport before you start – the quality of the relationship has been found to be *THE* most important element in getting results. So if nothing else, ask yourself at least two questions; do I like them, and more importantly, do I find them and their skills credible.

Whether or not you decide to engage the services of a professional, having a clear and compelling vision will be a great antidote to events in the past, which were negative, and enable you to focus on the things that are important to you now.

CHAPTER FIVE

Think BIG and set your vision

"If you don't build your dream someone will hire you to help build theirs."

~ **TONY GASKINS**

Finding meaning in life

The traditional assumption has been that when a person has a life they consider gives them meaning, it then leads to increased levels of well-being and overall happiness. Whether one causes the other or vice-versa, still seems an unanswered question. No matter! Be practical, and do both! From a state of happiness it's likely that you'll find meaning. Before you settle into create your vision, find something that is guaranteed to lift your spirits: listening to music, watch a favourite YouTube clip or if you have more time, watch an uplifting movie. You can look at your favourite pictures or take some form of physical activity, like taking a walk.

It's important for you to think big

Vision matters. Your vision or your destination matters. Often people describe the journey as being more important than the destination – and I think that's true AFTER you've set your direction. You set direction by having vision.

Mistake *Most people don't have a clear and compelling vision.*

TIP **Have a compelling vision that you can work towards. If you're not clear on what this is, then who can help you achieve it?**

If you work for yourself you may have set goals when you started out in business. Ask yourself:

- When did I achieve my goals, or when did I last review my goals?

- When were my goals last updated?

- Who's pushing me?

Sometimes people don't set their vision, and the reason given is the desire to keep one's options open. (The fallacy of keeping your options open was described in Chapter 1.) Don't become a drifter at the mercy of tides and winds. Set direction, and be clear on your course. Don't flounder. It may feel slightly risky but it's necessary. It is less risky than trying to stay still with the world moving past you.

"A ship in a harbour is safe, that is not what ships are built for."

~ GRACE HOPPER

I'm not suggesting that you have to do the thinking on your own. You do have to own it and take responsibility for it. Great athletes don't do it alone, they have a coach to push them further than they might push themselves. I'll talk more in Chapter 14 about working with an unreasonable friend to support, push and encourage you.

Ask yourself:

- Who do I 'report' to? Do I currently think they give me appropriate challenges?

How big is big?

It is our light not our darkness that most frightens us
Our deepest fear is not that we are inadequate.
Our deepest fear is that we are powerful beyond measure.
It is our light not our darkness that most frightens us.
We ask ourselves, who am I to be brilliant, gorgeous,
talented and fabulous?

~ MARIANNE WILLIAMSON

When setting your vision or destination, it has to be 'big', and by that I mean that it has to be an order of magnitude larger than where you are now. If we were talking money – put a nought on it, although I'm not necessarily talking money. You have already proven success – so for something to be a worthy challenge for you, your next step has to be significantly bigger than where you are now. It has to take you out of your comfort zone. The more successful you are, the larger your comfort zone, and therefore the challenges you set for yourself have to be larger too!

You know you have chosen a goal big enough when it is both exciting and scary!

For many people setting large goals can seem audacious. Indeed, Jim Collins talks in the business context about setting good "big hairy audacious goals or BHAGs" (pronounced Bee-hags).[10] Although your goals should be clear and compelling, they've not been randomly plucked from thin air.

Figure 5 over, shows the three elements that go into creating a BHAG. First is passion – something that you love to do. Secondly, it's something you're good at, and typically it will also include an element of financial compensation – or being paid for it. BHAGs are found at the intersection of what you're passionate about, what you could be the best in the world at and finding clear ways of monetising it.

Where BHAGS come from

Figure 5 – *Finding your audacious goal*

Chapter 4 explored what you enjoy and what you've been successful at, which also implies an element of monetary success. This chapter explores the element of passion.

I'll be giving you ways to find your passion. So many people have misplaced their passion – I'll spend some time suggesting ways for you to re-connect with it. Before you do any of it, here are a couple of words on the creative process, which can be important for many predominant left brain logicians to make sense of the process.

Left brain, right brain

You're probably aware that the brain is an organ of two halves. Each side of the brain controls different mental functions as well as different sides of our body. Although we have access to both parts of our brain, it seems that we favour one side over the other. Using our non-preferred side can feel awkward and unnatural, but that doesn't mean that you shouldn't use it. It's like using a muscle – if you don't use it, it will atrophy – and to achieve transformational results you'll want to be using BOTH sides of your brain.

The research has found that those who excel at activities requiring logic and sequence use more of their left brain. Those who use more of their right brain tend to prefer pictures / colours and whole systems thinking. There's been a bit of a debate over which is side is 'best', and whether both sides of the brain are necessary to be successful. Of course neither side is 'better', they're just different. Daniel Pink suggests the time has come for us to use our **whole** brain – and success will come to those who can use both sides of their brain.[11]

Dreaming can be a right brain activity, and may not seem natural for many people, so what follows is a 'how to' guide for allowing yourself to dream, and set your vision.

Set the stage for thinking big

"There is no passion to be found playing small – in settling for a life that is less than the one you are capable of living."

~ NELSON MANDELA

This section is a bit about how to set the stage for thinking big. Often the first step in thinking big is the initial idea. However, have you ever noticed how easy it is to shoot holes in ill-formed ideas – whether they are your own or others'? Or perhaps you know someone 'full of ideas', who just isn't practical. Ideas can get a bit of a bad name – but they need time to develop and grow.

I sometimes find it helpful to see ideas like small seedlings that need a bit of nurturing. When they're a bit more robust it does the seedlings good to be acclimatised to the outside in which to build their resilience. For ideas, there's an appropriate time to receive the constructive feedback – it's not in the very early stages – nurture your ideas, and gently acclimatise them to criticism and other people.

Three stage thinking for creativity

The following strategy is similar to one that *Walt Disney* adopted in the early days of the company. There are three essential aspects of the creative process. These aspects are: Dreamer, Planner and Critic. Dreamers have the ideas. Planners put the plans in place to make the dreams happen, and the Critics look for flaws in the plans and ideas.

Walt Disney had a strategy for keeping his 'creative' and 'ideas' people (Dreamers) away from the organisation's critics (see figure 6). He would ask his Dreamers to come up with ideas. The Dreamers would communicate with Planners to look at turning ideas into reality. The Planners would give the plans to Critics, who would look at all the places the plan could go wrong, and return to the Planners to fix. If the Planners could not fix it, they would ask the Dreamer for creative insight to come up with a creative way to solve the problem. Importantly, at no point do the Dreamer and Critic communicate directly, they do so via the Planner.

Three stage thinking for creativity

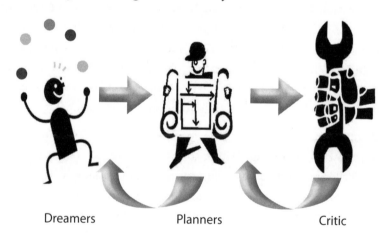

| Dreamers | Planners | Critic |

Figure 6 – *Keeping your critic separate*

Although *Walt Disney* apparently had three different types of people: Dreamers, Planners and Critics within us we each have the capability to do each type of thinking. Different thinking favours different parts of the brain. It might be that we've used some aspects of our 'self' more than others, and not surprisingly each may be developed to a different level of strength – but they're all there. It's highly likely that you will find at least one a little rusty and this then becomes another good opportunity for you to stretch your comfort zone, get into the growth mindset and engage with the process.

So that you don't stifle your own creativity I recommend you adopt the same disciplined approach that *Walt Disney* adopted in separating Dreamer from Critic. Don't allow your inner critic to spoil the ideas created by the dreaming part of you. I know you'll be concerned about duff ideas which you'll want to weed out, and in this respect timing is key. First, have the idea – have many ideas. Allow your ideas to develop, get some plans in place, *then* look at how to make the plans even more robust by directing your inner critic to find the implementation problems that the planner or dreamer can fix.

However, first a warning: people grow through stretching their comfort zones. This stretching is not always enjoyable. There's a sense of fumbling, uncertainty, and there can be fear – "can I do this?" and "what will the result look like?" For many people growth is neither an overnight nor a magic process – it is on-going. There are occasions when growth can be instantaneous – sadly most of the time, that's not the case. Growth takes energy and commitment. However, consider for a moment the alternative: stagnation which drains energy – both your own and the energy of those around you. At these times it will be important to keep in mind your vision and your very next step, which will help to keep you motivated.

Creating your vision

 Many people don't allow themselves to have ideas; they 'self-edit', and no sooner than the idea passes their lips, they cross it out, by saying "that'll never work".

 Separate your idea generation from the other stages – if necessary only do one stage per day.

This section is about dreaming. Where do you come up with your creative ideas – and apart from the shower – where else? During the course of this section, spend some time in your creative spot, listen to some uplifting music as I described earlier, and put aside your own Planner and Critic – their time will come. As you dream, if you hear the voice of either, then be gentle in your recognition. For example: "Ah, my inner critic; how lovely for you to want to support me. But not now; your time will come later."

If you don't have a dream for yourself, who will?

The following approaches have things in common. They encourage you to be free of constraints (remember the tethered piglet from Chapter 1). Constraints can come from many different places, including upbringing and being told things like "it's rude to ask". Each of these techniques seeks to overcome the constraints without exploring why they're there. I would imagine there were good reasons for the pig to be tethered to the stake in the same way that you've inherited constraints. All I'm interested in here is showing you how to break free of what's holding you back.

You may also notice that dreaming doesn't yet include *how* you're going to achieve your dreams – that comes later as part of Planner. I've heard it said to keep focusing on the dream for at least three weeks before focusing on how you might start to achieve it. If, when you get to the activity and you think or begin to write something, you hear yourself saying anything critical such as "that will never work", or "that's not me" or maybe "gosh, I wouldn't know where to start with that one", remember this is entirely normal – for you it's likely that you're exercising a less used part of your brain – so congratulate yourself for putting in the effort, and for now, put those thoughts to one side and keep writing (or drawing) **what you do want? What's your dream?**

Become one of the 'crazy ones'

"Those who are crazy enough to think they can change the world, usually do."

~ **Anon**

The distribution curve of the population, numbers of people against developmental level suggests levels of development from sub-mediocrity through to mediocrity, on to possibility and finally 'evolving' into becoming one of the 'crazy ones' (see figure 7). The names of these stages are not meant to be derogatory in any way, but to show the natural advancement. Each stage can evolve to the next, unless of course they get stuck.

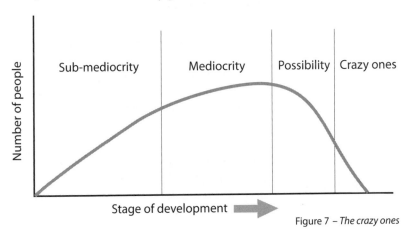

Figure 7 – *The crazy ones*

A 'crazy one' is someone who is inspirational – they inspire others. If you want to raise your game and, if you want transformational results, then the challenge is for you to aspire to and become one of the crazy ones. That's my wish for you. To find your dream, and therefore a challenge that gives you more than enough meaning in your life to break free of constraints of ordinary life and to experience an extra-ordinary life. What's your wish for yourself?

I suspect that you want it too. I reach that conclusion because you've bought this book about how to raise your game and achieve transformational results. The book is founded on the premise that you've already tasted success. Your previous success means it more likely that you're currently living in 'possibility', and your next evolution is "to become a crazy one".

I realise talk of personal evolution could be a little contentious; however there is significant research supports the idea of different developmental stages in adults. One example, in Table 1 below, from leadership theory and practice describes different stages of development of a leader. People can and do develop through the different stages.[12]

	Characterised by:
The Alchemist	*The ability to reinvent themselves and their organisations in historically significant ways. An extraordinary capacity to deal simultaneous ways with many situations at multiple levels. Deal with priorities and long-term goals.*
The Strategist	*Focus on organisational constraints and perceptions, which they see as discussable and transformable. Adept at creating shared visions. Highly effective change agents.*

The Individualist	*Tend to ignore rules they see as irrelevant; can be seen as a bit of a wild-card.*
The Achiever	*Create a positive work environment, and focus on deliverables – often lack "outside the box" thinking.*
The Expert	*Exercise control by perfecting their knowledge.*
The Diplomat	*Loyally serves, and pleases higher status colleagues. Avoids conflict.*
The Opportunist	*Mistrust, egocentrism and manipulativeness.*

Table 1 – *Stages of Leadership (Rooke & Torbert, 2005)*

My intention behind this book is to inspire you to achieve the highest level. The levels can't be skipped. They are progressed through sequentially, each developmental level integrating knowledge from previous levels.

Ways to start dreaming:

I've found that some people have difficulty getting started on the dreaming process. So what follows are different approaches; read through them all and start with one. The first one is the longest taking upwards of twenty minutes, whereas the others are quicker ideas to stimulate your thinking, and they have elements of similarity – encouraging you to be free of constraints. After you've read them, give yourself at least 40 minutes of uninterrupted time for this activity.

- Best Possible Self
- Blurt
- Parallel universe
- Role model
- Champion
- Repetition
- Enjoyment
- Designer life
- Working at your best

Best Possible Self

One researched and documented approach is to first spend about twenty to thirty minutes imagining your best possible self, and to think about what you expect your life to be in one to ten years from now.[13] Visualise a future for yourself in which everything has turned out the way you wanted; you put effort in, and worked to achieve all your goals. Remember it takes no more effort to visualise big goals and achievements. Having taken time to visualise, put in writing what you have imagined. This step of putting it in writing is important.

Blurt

Say, unedited what comes to mind when you think about your vision. You can record yourself 'Blurt' or just pour your thoughts on to a large A3 piece of paper, either in words or on a mindmap. What do you want to be, do, have or give? How do you want to live your life in the next year, five years or even in ten years time?

You live in a parallel universe

One approach that I've found works may initially sound a little odd. The idea is to liberate you from constraints of reality. Later you can explore what's real and what's changed (like the pig from Chapter 1).

If you can imagine another you, living on a parallel universe – how are they living in an idealised world? You may remember a TV advert with two versions of the same couple driving a car, who meet at the traffic lights. One version of the couple is in a nicer car, and better dressed. If you existed in another place where you're living to your maximum potential –what is the premium version of you, and what are you known for?

Role model

Who's a famous person from history whose qualities you admire – what are their qualities? How do these relate to your qualities? How can you develop these qualities? What could you do to have these qualities 'more' in your life?

Becoming a champion

What's a 'cause' that you want to champion? Given you've already achieved success – this is likely to be a cause larger than your immediate family – perhaps it's within your local community or even bigger still, a societal challenge where you could make a difference. My 'cause' is to enable others to become even more successful.

What's your mission? What can you do with the gifts, skills and experiences that you have?

All work involves elements of repetition – what do you want to repeat?

All work involves some element of repetition whether the factory worker or CEO. Even the seemingly glamorous work of becoming an actress seems to involve repetition – there are retakes on set, and then countless interviews answering similar questions.

What bits of life or your work do you enjoy repeating?

What do you enjoy?

What do you enjoy, at home or work? If you could do some of that everyday ... what would that be?

Designer life

Design your ideal day or a week. How do you spend your time? What do you do? Who would you be doing it with? Where are you working?

How do you work best?

Do you prefer collaborating with others or working alone?

Do you work best in a structured way, where the goal is clearly defined? Perhaps you prefer flexibility and are energised by last minute activities. Do you prefer to respond to demands? Do you like sorting out the details, or maybe you have a sense of how things fit together within a larger scheme.

Structured dreaming

One of the things I noticed with clients is that sometimes structure can aid the creativity process, and it can also give 'permission' to 'want' things in different areas of our life. I think for some people it balances material desires with goals contributing to the greater good.

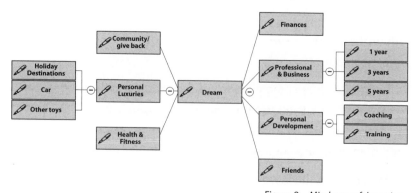

Figure 8 – *Mind map of dreaming*

I recommend starting a dream mind map with different branches reflecting different areas of your life.

Use colours

Use of colours and mind maps are often more natural for people used to using their right brain. I suggest *you* use colours for your mind map, and if this feels unnatural for you GREAT – this is another opportunity for you to get outside your comfort zone – and start to GROW. As you do this task, positively feel new neural networks being formed in the brain – which will of course need significant repetition to create the amounts of repetition needed for expertise status – but you've started the process.

Remember this is still a blurt – so allow yourself to put anything and everything down at this stage. Remember – if you hear the voice "that's too big" "or that's not appropriate" – thank and quieten the voice. What you're experiencing is very normal. You can edit later.

OK, that's the overview of the different ways to do this task. Give yourself 40 minutes for this activity; long enough for creativity to come. Write it down. Ideally, coloured pens and paper will do the trick. When you notice ideas slowing down – change the colour of your pen and continue.

Many people distract themselves from their dreams by searching for mind-mapping software for their computer. Then learning how to use it ... going through the phase of it being 'too hard', and 'giving up' attributing the difficulty to the dreaming process. I don't want this to be you – so, forgive me shouting ...

"Get on with it!   Use PEN AND PAPER!" If you like the mind-mapping process – you can find software in the future.

OK! You've completed this. Well done! Sleep on it.

Review

After you have left your initial ideas for at least 24 hours, you can go back and review – it's important to note that this is not yet moving to the Planning stage, this is more a refinement, adding big chunks that occur to you or adding some detail to make it more compelling. There may be some things to look up and add specifics. You want a holiday – where? What sort of accommodation? What do you want to do whilst you're there?

As you look at your dream output, ask yourself: "What am I pleased with? What has surprised me? Is there anything that jars with me? How clearly does it say what I want?"

Dream board

Having created the structure you can start to develop a pictorial dream board. One of the benefits of this is that you put it where you can see it, on a daily basis. Traditionally this was a large piece of paper with pictures snipped from magazines. Alternatively, you could create a screen saver with your dreams. However, with the advent of reasonably priced electronic photo frames and, the ease of being able to find specific pictures on the internet, this is my recommendation. Create the dream board in an electronic photo frame, and put it where you can see it – DAILY.

Dream boards are a very visual medium, and not everyone has preference for taking in information visually. You take information in though all five senses of: sight, sound, feel, smell and taste. To immerse yourself in your dream you can also devise ways of appealing to other senses. I'm not sure that it's possible to devise a tasty and aromatic meal that represents my dreams through the senses of taste and smell – although I don't have Heston Blumental's creative culinary streak, perhaps you do.

On the raiseyourgame.biz website there is a short questionnaire, which you can use to determine your preferred style for taking in information – and use to think about the best way to present your ideas to yourself.

To appeal to your sense of hearing, you can create statements, which represent your ideas.

Many people don't pay attention to the words that they use, and the actual meaning, or they're vague rather than specific.

Ensure that you write your statements in the current tense, and say them out loud on a daily basis. This has long been suggested as an effective way to achieve your success.[14]

One client wrote: "I am in demand for my skills."
Perhaps coincidentally, the following week several of his acquaintances wanted big chunks of his time. He quickly realised he'd missed the element of compensation for his time. His amended statement read "I'm in demand for my skills and receive excellent payment." Although he continued to be willing to support his friends, he wanted to be clear that he intended the statement to mean that he was in demand by his clients.

Not all visualisation leads to results

For many years I've found short visualisations to be effective with groups and individuals. While doing some research on different ways of visualising, I discovered a couple of really important pieces of information that are often overlooked. Firstly, don't just focus on achieving the goal, it's important to focus too on overcoming obstacles.[15] Secondly, don't get too carried away by experiencing the fantasy of the visualisation, you haven't achieved your goals – be sure to come back to reality – and be ready to take action![16]

Visualisation

Often when people visualise they like to close their eyes, although it's not essential. Many people 'see' the picture and find it easiest to start with that. If you find it easier, you can start with the sounds or feelings of success, and if you can include all three (sights, sounds and feelings), then that's ideal. Some people include tastes or smells – but that is more unusual. Hold the picture in your mind's eye. Then work back; visualise yourself preparing for your goal in a way that will lead to maximum success. It's important to see yourself making step-by-step progress towards meeting your goal.

If you prefer, you can listen to an audio file of me reading these steps, which is available on raiseyourgame.biz/downloads, so that you can immerse yourself in the visualisation.

If you're ready to close your eyes, do it now. Take a couple of deep breaths. Very good. Take a moment to think about what success means to you. Visualise success! What do you see? What else? Who's there with you? Brighten the colours for a moment. You may have to turn the sound up – tune in to what they're saying – listen well. What else do you hear? Listen some more. Good. Now notice your feelings in this successful place. Notice any significant textures? Good. What's the taste of success? Now take an extra moment to notice any significant smells? Now you have that visualisation, hold it for a moment. Good.

Think back to the things you've done to achieve your success. What are some of the obstacles that you have overcome to get to where you are now? What are some of your key inner resources that allowed you to overcome these obstacles? What else? Now think of some of the practical things that you did to get where you are, and achieve your success. What did you do? What else? Who else supported you in your endeavours? How did you get them involved? How did you prioritise your time? Take as long as you need to absorb the key learnings. Good. And when you're ready, and only when you are ready, gently bring your awareness back to the room and open your eyes.

Before moving on to the next activity (either in the book or in life), take a moment to pause and reflect on what you've visualised.

What next?

You must stay focused on what you want.

I mentioned that there are three approaches to thinking: Dreamer, Planner and Critic. I've deliberately stopped at Dreamer, with you having created your vision. I will come back to the Planning piece in Chapter 12 when I describe goal setting. Goal setting is a useful piece in knowing the first steps to turn your vision into reality BUT there's something useful about 'sitting with' your vision: just live with it, to allow your vision to fully germinate, to gain strength without yet knowing how it's going to be achieved.

Sharing your dreams

It can be very useful to have a person to bounce ideas off, and one way you can help the process is being clear as to what you'd like, at least initially from the other person. Are you looking to develop the idea, or have you moved into the planning stage, or are you asking them to assist in anticipating problems with the turning it into reality. The other aspect is timing of when you share your ideas.

Mistake *Many people share their vision too soon, only to have their ideas crushed.*

TIP **In the early stages, visions need incubation nurturing, and a little time.**

> I have a very good friend who has an exceptionally strong critic. Several years ago, I found that no sooner than an idea would leave my mouth, she would 'trample on it' describing all the reasons it wouldn't work. Fortunately, I noticed my reluctance at sharing my ideas with her – and with honest communication and flexibility by both parties, we were able to sort it out.

Not everyone is able to adapt their approach, so you may choose not to share your personal ideas with some people until your ideas are a little more robust.

In group situations (for example brainstorming, or collaboration sessions) where ideas need to be created and developed the approach is different. Share ideas early and have the group mould the idea in order to get group buy-in and ownership. It's useful to set clear boundaries at the outset, that everyone is in Dreamer mode together, and set clear distinctions between each of the stages in the Three Stage Thinking for Creativity process.

Working with others on their dreams

If you're working with others on their ideas, it can be useful to be explicit with the Three Stage Thinking for Creativity. I'm not suggesting that you don't share your constructive insights, although timing of your intervention is key.

CHAPTER SIX

Values, your inner compass

"Things that matter most should never be at the mercy of things that matter least."

~ GOETHE

What are values?

This chapter is about becoming more consciously aware of your values. Your values are (implicit or internal) criteria by which you make decisions. Your values and value differences can cause both inner conflict, and indecisiveness. Knowing what your values are can help you design a life that allows yourself to *live to the maximum,* according to your values.

Many people 'put off' decisions. This 'putting off' can sometimes happen because of conflicting values, which leads to a lack of clarity over priorities. The outcome is indecisiveness and wasted mental energy. Progress towards transformational results isn't made whilst decisions are held in limbo. Procrastination won't get you transformational results.

Many people don't know their values, the criteria by which they make decisions.

Know your values, in order to take timely decisions, which are aligned to what's important to you.

In order to raise your game you want your background mental processing power to be focused on achieving transformational results. Consistent decision making and taking the appropriate action in alignment with your vision will take you closer to achieving results.

Therefore, being explicitly aware of your values puts you in more control of your decision making. When you understand what's important – your priorities and your values – you can then make decisions more easily.

Why are values important?

We all have values; each of us is likely to hold a slightly (or significantly) different set of values. Explicitly knowing your values can be very powerful. By knowing your values it is easier to make choices, and steer a course through life. Values are like having a compass pointing out the direction to follow. You have to have the route planned (your vision) first, but your values will keep you heading in the ultimate direction – even if you get blown off course.

Values are a way of understanding differences with people, and they are used in decision making, whether you're aware of it or not.

Let's take a practical look at your values in a particular context. You have some core values that are true in many different contexts – however, values can change depending on the situation.

What car do you drive?

What car do you drive? Think for a moment how you came to choose it. Take a moment to recall the criteria you used to make your choice. Even if you didn't go through a huge decision making process, it could be that even that decision reflects your values – perhaps efficiency in decision making is a value, or it's just a low priority.

When coaching two business associates, I asked them about what was important to them in their choice of car. One of them talked about luxury and comfort, and the other talked about image and speed.

Does it surprise you that I subsequently found out that one drove a Lexus, and the other a Porsche. One key point to note from this short example is that values can be different for different people, and influence our choices. One person valued luxury and comfort and the other person valued image and speed; these are their values, which guided their decision making process, and for the two associates the difference in values went further than just the cars they drove.

Values in conflict

For example, someone who has a values of 'making a difference' and 'family' may sometimes find themselves torn between making a difference to the wider society or spending time at home with family.

Another example I often see is business owners who want to be in control (of everything), and also have a value around growth. Sometimes it's important to let go of total control in order to make space for growth.

Values in setting direction

For many people exploring their values can be powerful in setting their direction. Often in life there are a number of things that we think that we 'should' do, or 'ought' to do. What is similar in 'shoulds' and 'oughts' is that they come from someone else's agenda – not yours. Discovering your values ensures that the things that you do are consciously part of what you *want* to be doing, and how you want to be investing your time and energy.

Values as a way of explaining interpersonal differences

If you have a great team, it's likely that you've unwittingly recruited people with similar values. As the 'boss', often what you say goes, so it's possible that you only rarely experience a values conflict. This isn't necessarily a good thing as it's useful to have someone to challenge your thinking.

However, as you continue to raise your game, develop your business and form strategic new relationships, it's useful to know your values and what you stand for. You can then be on the lookout to find suitable strategic partners who have complementary values. A strategic partnership based on aligned values is more likely to lead to success, rather than one where your time and energy is focused on ironing out continual misunderstandings and going off in different directions. Differences in values can help to explain slight differences in opinions ... all the way through to conflict.

How to find your values

Go to http://**raiseyourgame.biz/** and print and cut out the value cards.

In the download there are five scale cards – with words ranging from very important, important to not very important. There are also 45 value cards, most with words and a brief description, and a couple of blanks in case there's a specific value you would like to add.

Finding your values can take anywhere between 10–40 minutes, and it will be time well invested. Find somewhere where you won't be interrupted, and I strongly suggest you sit on the floor. Sitting in a more child-like position disconnects you from the 'should' and 'oughts' and is more likely to connect you to what's really important. 'Obligations' that come from 'should' and 'oughts' are more likely to arise from sitting at your desk – or even the kitchen table.

1. Choose the context (e.g. business) that you want to find your values.

2. Put the scale cards in order.

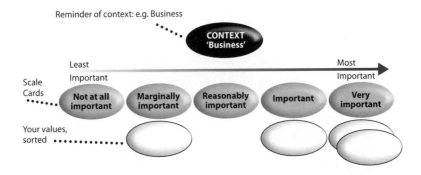

Figure 9 – *Initial Values Sort*

3. Take a values card, read it, and then use your gut instinct to put it in one of the piles. Take just a couple of seconds (per card and even if you're a slower reader, I suggest no more than 30 seconds per card).

4. Repeat for all of the cards. By the end the cards should be distributed across the piles, reflecting which your strongest values are.

Great – that's the *initial* part done. It can be useful to take a moment to make a note of your first impressions of the list of values in your most important pile? Overall, is there anything that surprises you?

In a moment I'll ask you to prioritise what's in your 'very important' pile – and here are a few words on the benefits of doing so.

Your private values masterclass

By investing a little time now "getting down and dirty" with your values, the benefit is twofold: firstly, you will gain clarity over aspects of your own indecisiveness; secondly, you will begin to see how any changes to your values have a larger knock-on effect with those around you.

The values cycle

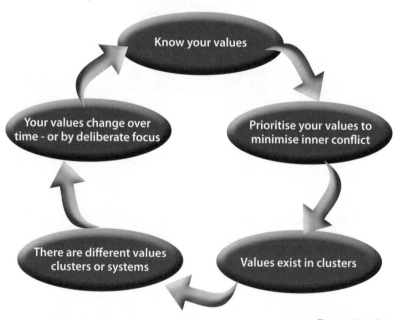

Figure 10 – *Values*

The diagram shows the cyclic nature of values. Knowing your values is the first step, which you've now done for one area of your life. Next you can prioritise your values so that you can minimise inner conflict, and reach decisions more easily. Decisions lead to action, and actions lead to results.

Prioritising your values

Having found your values, it can be useful to prioritise. More than eight 'top' criteria becomes slightly unwieldy in decision making – so if you do have more than eight in your 'very important' pile – go through them and find the top eight. Having worked with hundreds of people in this activity, I've found that different ways work for different people.

OPTION 1:

You might find it really easy to put your values in a hierarchical sequence, and move a couple of your values from the 'very important' pile to the 'important' pile. Remember they're still your values – what you're looking for here are your top eight in the particular context you chose.

OPTION 2:

You might find that there's a way you can combine similar values, perhaps in a new word, or perhaps one word represents similar aspects, thus reducing the number of discrete items.

OPTION 3:

If neither of the above work for you and you'll benefit from going through a sequenced approach to find your priorities – the instructions might look off putting – but essentially you're just comparing two values at a time and deciding which of the two has the highest importance to you in a particular context.

How to prioritise your values when they all look 'very important'

1. Take one value and place it on the table / floor.

2. Take the next value and ask yourself, which is the more important of the two, and place it higher or lower.

3. Take your third value; compare it against the highest value of these two values. Which is the most important? If it is higher than the first value, place it above it. If not, compare to the next value down. If it is higher, insert it between; if it is lower, place it underneath.

4. Repeat steps 2 and 3 with all the values in your 'very important' pile. By the end of this activity you will have a hierarchy for your values in a particular context.

5. Write them down with a date (remember values change, and it can be frustrating to look back, and not remember when you last looked at your values).

Once you've found *your* values, you can start to envisage what "living *your* life to the max" would look like for each value. What would you be doing now, which you're not already? This is where your values can start to provide valuable insight and direction.

Everyone has values, and these values can be different. Starting the process of understanding these differences can give you useful information when working with others.

Value Clusters and Orphans: The cause of inner turmoil

It's been shown that values exist in clusters. If we have certain values, then it's likely that we'll hold values in different and related areas.[17] These values are represented in a chart. Where values sit close to one another there's not likely to be as much conflict as where the values are opposite.

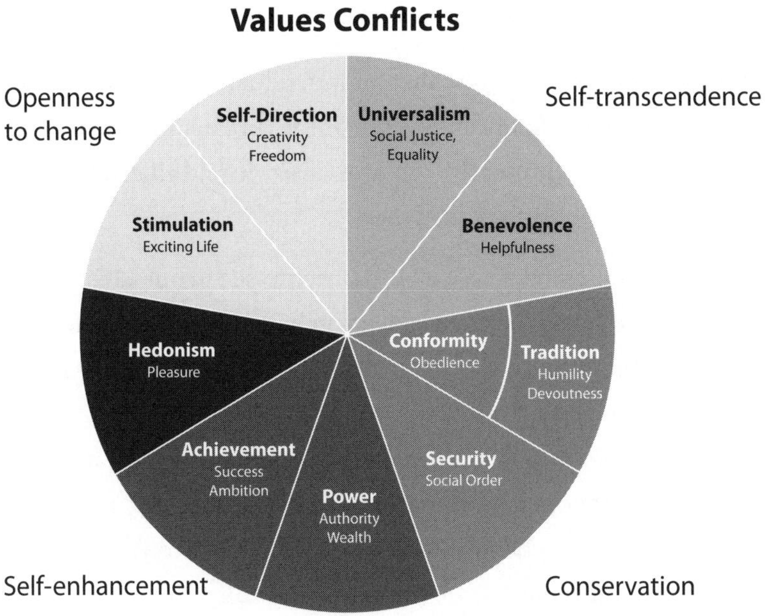

Values Conflicts

Openness
to change

Self-transcendence

Self-Direction
Creativity
Freedom

Universalism
Social Justice,
Equality

Stimulation
Exciting Life

Benevolence
Helpfulness

Hedonism
Pleasure

Conformity
Obedience

Tradition
Humility
Devoutness

Achievement
Success
Ambition

Security
Social Order

Power
Authority
Wealth

Self-enhancement

Conservation

Figure 11 – *Values (Schwartz, 2005)*

For example, someone with values around security, is more likely to also have values around the importance of authority, tradition and perhaps conformity, and is less likely to hold values around living an exciting life.

It's easy to see how different people might hold different values. For example, the local shop owner who's been trading from the same premises for 23 years and who probably values tradition is not the same as an entrepreneur starting new businesses in different industries and on different continents who enjoys the exciting life.

However, if you have values on opposite sides, then this 'clash' might cause inner conflict, because you're striving for different things. Using the above example if you value security, and also want an exciting life you can see that this is likely to cause you some internal conflict. This conflict is normal, and knowing how you can deal with it will begin to lead you to transformational results.

Your values can change over time

There's evidence to suggest that an individual's values change over time. Sometimes significant events or life threatening events cause us to see things differently – you've heard it said that this type of event causes people to reprioritise.

Often changes in values can be harder to see in ourselves. Values can be like our taste in music, it can change without us noticing. You probably have music from your youth, or a TV programme that you found amazing 'back then' and when you see the re-run, or hear the album now it doesn't quite live up to expectations. It's easy to think that music or plotlines have evolved – but so have you – your values have changed, and will continue to evolve as you raise your game and achieve transformational results.

Value systems

Not surprisingly people who share similar sets (clusters) of values 'get on. Often when you look at people with different value systems their values might seem misguided. However, a little like the developmental stages I described in Chapter 5 it seems that the stages are hierarchical, each stage encompasses the previous stage, and stages can't be skipped.

Spiral Dynamics is a value systems approach based on the work of Dr Graves.[18] Each stage is given a colour, and there's an upward spiral, going from individual to group, back to individual to community – and on each upward spiral having an expanded set of values. The key point to note from the table below is that these different value systems exist. You might recognise your values system, but it's not essential.

Here's a summary:

Colour	Brief description	Values
Turquoise	Global	Synergy, integration
Yellow	System / Choice seeker	Exploration, freedom, flexibility, independence, self-worth, balance
Green	Humanity / Involver	Idealism, equality, cooperation, harmony, acceptance, consensus
Orange	Competence / Achieving	Opportunity, competence, achievement, variety
Blue	Order / loyalist	Stability, security, discipline, duty, truth, honesty, fairness, consistency
Red	Power / loner	Power, risk, control, self-reliance, respect
Purple	Tribal / clan	Safety, family, tradition
Beige	Survival	Survival, instinct

Table 2 – *Value Systems (Spiral Dynamics)*

You can deliberately adjust your values

"The significant problems we face cannot be solved at the same level of thinking we were at when we created them."

~ ALBERT EINSTEIN

It's OK not to want to make big changes to your values; actually, it's OK not to make any change. However, if you do decide that you want to make some changes, think about the support network that you will need.

Many people don't join new groups, or develop new relationships to support them in achieving the change in values to support their transformational results.

The importance of getting new stimulus through new groups is discussed more in Chapter 10, and Chapter 14 describes benefits of external support, such as a coach.

One way of changing your thinking is to keep a growth mindset. Another way is to change your thinking is to deliberately adjust your values. Often significant life events or a health scare cause people to re-evaluate their values. Don't wait for a negative event to give you a kick up the butt; you can re-evaluate your values *without* a significant life event, through conscious attention in order to raise your game and achieve transformational results.

There's research available to show that world views and our value systems do change, whilst the expectation is that this is a slow process, particular events can cause the change to be almost instantaneous.

CHAPTER SEVEN

Small changes, big impact

"If you think small things don't make a difference, you've never been in bed with a mosquito!"

~ ANITA RODDICK

Big changes, big impact

When you've had success, you are already somewhat of a master and it's likely that you already have many good practices in place.

Earlier we explored the importance of maintaining a growth mindset in continuing to be open to new opportunities. You've started the process of developing and refining your clear and compelling vision, both mindset and vision are key elements to propel you forward. You might have found that reconnecting with your values 'reprioritises' or refocuses you on what's important to you now. These are some of the key things that can make a big impact. However, in this chapter we'll explore the importance of making small deliberate changes.

Small changes, big impact

It's often easy to dismiss the importance of making small changes, thinking they won't make a significant difference. However, nothing could be further from the truth; small changes can have a big impact. First, I'd like to explore a couple of charts showing the incredible difference small changes can have.

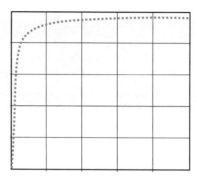

Figure 12 - *Mastery*

Mastery

First of all take a look at the graph of mastery. The curved line shows the development of skill over time. At the beginning of learning any new skill there's the opportunity for massive changes, which tapers, then slows quite rapidly.

Let's take the earlier example of learning to drive. In seventeen weeks, I went from complete beginner to having passed my driving test. My driving skills have improved since taking my test, although not at the same initial rate. What this means is, the more skilled you've become, learning new skills have seemingly less impact on your overall skills.

However, there are different skills to be gained. I use the term 'skills' in the broadest possible sense. You probably have a great set of 'technical' skills, and there are a broader set of skills to be gained. Michael Gerber in *The E-Myth Revisited* described the three different roles that an owner manager typically takes on within his business: the Technician, the Manager and the Entrepreneur.[19]

Gerber describes how most businesses are started by technicians, people with the specific technical skills to do the job. Therefore,

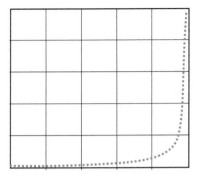

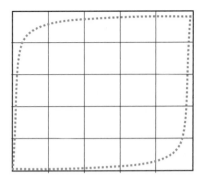

Figure 13 - *Results*

Figure 14 - *Superimposed*

if you've come from the technical background the likelihood is that you already have the technical skills for your role. However, to raise your game you might want to consider developing some complementary skills. What about your skills of 'manager' and 'entrepreneur' – perhaps you are further to the left on the curve – and developing your skills here will have enormous impact. This is returned to later in this chapter.

Income

Let's compare the graph of mastery (figure 12) with the graph of success (figure 13). The dotted line on this graph plots income distribution, but it can be any measure of success.[20] For a long time results are relatively small, and then the results start to massively increase.

Take a look at the graphs superimposed (figure 14). It really is that last square where the difference happens; on the mastery graph the line in the last box shows no discernible change. However, on the results graph, the box on the right is where all the action happens, and transformational results occur. How many people do you know who change what they do, or start a new game before results kick in?

Many people don't wait for the harvest, before becoming captivated by starting something new.

With the success you've had, you're already *so close* to achieving transformational results. So, how do you find the difference that makes the difference? It's not one big thing. Imagine making 100 small adjustments, each one contributing to just a 1% improvement. That will give *at least* 100% improvement. During the London Olympics I heard the expression the 'aggregation of marginal gains', as applied to the British Olympic Cycling team. No single thing made the difference, but the culmination of many small changes has led to domination in the sport.

Change is cumulative, like interest rates in the bank. Technically *less than* 100 changes will be needed for 100% improvement. For example, to double one's capital with a bank paying 1% interest per year, it's likely to take 70 years. Unlike the bank example, you're not limited to one change per year. Making just one change per week, takes less than 2 years to make 100% improvement. On your journey to achieve transformational results, how quickly you implement the changes are up to you!

You might be ready to start something new, and you might want to take some time to think about which skills you have which are transferable. They may not be the 'technical' skills, perhaps they're the skills of management or entrepreneurship that you can build upon. You're not necessarily starting from scratch.

Monitoring changes

Perhaps the above information is compelling enough for you to go out and make lots of changes.

 Many people make lots of random changes without learning from the change.

You are a human being and also a 'human system' and changes in one aspect of the system will have impacts in other areas. In order to make the most of the changes, you have to be an observer to the changes. You wouldn't put oil in a car without monitoring the correct level. Too much oil can be as destructive to your car as too little oil.

Let's explore the 'human system' so that you can monitor the impact of change.

What you see is NOT what you get

You may have heard the expression WYSIWYG (pronounced whizy-wig), the translation being: what you see is what you get. The term once applied to graphics software, and meant that what was displayed on the screen was what was printed out – pretty commonplace with today's technology. The term WYSIWYG implied transparency, and nothing hidden. As human beings, we're not always WYSIWYG; there's more going on under the surface than meets the eye.

Iceberg

So that you get a sense of how small things are connected to bigger shifts in our sense of being, one way to think about a person is like an iceberg.[21] An iceberg only has one ninth sitting above the waterline; it's similar with a person.

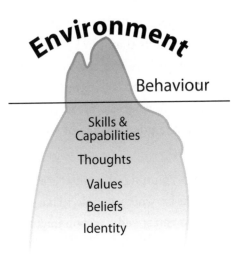

Figure 15 – *Iceberg*

Outside of our self is the environment. Our environment affects how we behave. Imagine for a moment if your office was painted, from floor to ceiling in black. Contrast this with a gentle shade of green? It's likely that most people would find the black oppressive and the green more calming. Just the change of colour in your environment is likely to impact your thoughts, which will affect behaviour.

What we see in others is their behaviour; what they do, what they say and how they say it and their actions on inaction in any situation. Whilst we might see the results of their skills and capabilities, we're unlikely to be familiar with their inner thoughts, or understand their values or beliefs.

For some people there's 'beyond identity' – not something we'll explore further in this book.

Even though we don't see people's thoughts, values or beliefs, they are interconnected and changes in one area impact other areas.

How thinking affects skills

How a person thinks will affect their skills and behaviours. If a person thinks they can be successful, then they're likely to act in a more positive way than if they think they can't. If you were to think the deal is 'way out of your league', you may not even submit a proposal, whereas if it were your ideal target market, you think you have a good chance of winning it, then you're likely to put in the effort.

Underpinning thoughts are values & beliefs. Values are the criteria by which people make decisions. Knowing your 'hidden' criteria can speed decision making. Beliefs are thoughts about the world that which we hold to be true. In the same way that values can change, so can beliefs. We discussed this in relation to the tethered pig, and crossing the road in Chapter 1. Another example of where beliefs change is children who believe in Santa Clause.

I've worked with a number of clients who believe it is rude to interrupt – on first examination this belief might look quite civilised – however the problems with beliefs is that they are rigid and don't allow for irregular events. They are often held by the individual as something like: "never interrupt anyone, ever". Such rigidity can lead to ineffectiveness when dealing with others.

Identity is who you are, rather than what you do. Throughout this book I've encouraged you to explore and upgrade your thoughts, values and beliefs to ensure that you have the latest version for success. However, your identity is yours and yours alone. You will do the work, and you will make the changes – that's down to you and your identity.

Changes are linked

All of the levels of the iceberg are linked. A change in one area of the iceberg can affect other areas. You want to achieve transformational results? The way you do this is by adjusting the system appropriately. Appropriately in this context means: with awareness. Once the change is made (or even suggested) it's useful to notice your thoughts and feelings to see what information this provides you and to see if you've got additional work on updating thoughts or beliefs.

This is especially important if you think that you can't or won't do something – there's rich learning to be had – which will probably equate to more than a 1% improvement in your results once you explore the relevancy and accuracy of your thoughts, values and beliefs.

Of course the first step is paying attention to your thoughts, to distinguish what they are, and where appropriate, to be able to challenge them if they're no longer serving you well.

> For example, one of my mentors, Dan Priestly set a challenge for me to carry £1000 in cash for a period of time. This is a small change in behaviour, right? I remember my initial thought was "I'm not the type of person who carries cash", certainly not what seemed like a significant amount of cash. This thought was more of an identity level statement. As soon as I noticed the thought, I became curious: why shouldn't I be the type of person who is comfortable with cash? What are my values and beliefs that might prevent me becoming that type of person ... and could I become that type of person? Did I want to become that type of person?

In business, just monitoring and observing can bring change. Just monitoring and observing thoughts can develop awareness – and there's no substitute for taking action.

So, where to start?

You can initiate change, and thus find different ways to raise your game at each of these different levels of the iceberg. Chapter 3 described the importance of having a growth mindset, which starts to explore your beliefs around your ability to change. Chapter 5 started to explore your current values and suggested that deliberate changes at this level can have profound effects.

Earlier in Chapter 1 I described the terms comfort zone and stretch zone. Success broadens our comfort zone – which is nice and comfortable – but doesn't lead us to growth. Growth typically happens in the stretch zone, which is by definition outside of your comfort zone. And remember that to maximise your opportunities for learning in your stretch zone, notice your thinking and challenge unhelpful beliefs or thoughts.

You can have a good look at your beliefs, the things that you hold to be true, and with a growth mindset scanning for new information you can start to question to see if any of your beliefs need a bit of an update.

How do you know if a thought is not helpful?

When you have a thought, it's very easy to take it for granted, to assume that it's true. However, you want to find thoughts and beliefs that are unhelpful and are holding you back, so it can be helpful to question your thoughts; are they really accurate in today's world as the person you are now? Are you still operating with 'rules' relevant for a five-year-old, with the skills, wisdom and experience of who you are now? Like my mountain biking colleague from Chapter 1, are you operating as if you need to put your feet on the ground when you'd have more power with updated beliefs? When have you tested the accuracy of the thought to see if it still holds true? What follows are some specific clues that you can listen out for that indicate that your thoughts are not helpful.

Generalisations

If you hear yourself using words like 'always' or 'never', then it's likely that you're making generalisations, which may mean you're missing out on some specific information. If you notice that generalising has become one of your habits, become an 'exception hunter'. Look for and find the exception – not to 'prove the rule', but to find evidence that there are very few things in life which 'always' happen. If you become tuned to find exceptions, it means that you're more likely to spot opportunities that others might miss. Especially if they think "nothing new ever happens in this industry".

Orders

Sometimes you might notice that your thoughts contain 'orders' about some of the things that you should, ought or must do (or think). For example, "you must ..." The positive is that they can make decisions easy, and the downside is that you might be doing things that are unnecessary just because you think you 'ought' to.

Again the first thing to do is to pay attention to your thoughts, and if you notice thought patterns which include the 'oughts', 'should' and 'musts', then you can start to question these external 'rules'. Why 'must' you be in the office every day? Who says you 'should' respond to every email.

Often these 'orders' can be similar to the generalisations, and they mean that you're not operating flexibly. Without flexibility, it might mean that you're missing out on opportunities to raise your game. In many situations it can be useful to loosen the rigidity around the belief.

http://raiseyourgame.biz contains a short belief change activity.

It ends in disaster

Some people become hamstrung because their thought patterns race to the "worst possible outcome". If you find when considering change that your brain races unprompted to "what if" scenarios with disastrous consequences, then the habit to break is that of catastrophisation.

The trick here is to write down the links in the chain. There is generally a pseudo logical set of links – make a note of them.

A common set of links is: If you invest in a new opportunity which turns out to be duff, you will lose your business and your home, you end up divorced, no access to the kids and living in a shelter for the homeless.

Then think about the likelihood of each step happening. Also consider alternative options at each stage.

Once you've gone through the disaster scenario, challenge yourself to come up with a "what if" in which it turns out that not only do you come up smelling of roses, but "save the day". Show the chain of events, and assign probabilities again. You will see that there's a pretty equal chance of both positive and negative events happening.

You can mitigate against risk, and put plans in place.

There are other common thinking traps:

- Jumping to conclusions on small amounts of information
- Inferring meaning where there is none
- Grandiose – making events larger than they are
- Discounting – not taking account of the full facts of the situation
- Putting self at the centre – it's all about me!
- It's never me!
- Mindreading – I think what you're thinking is …
- Taking emotions as data

Each of the thought patterns can become so ingrained that we don't easily see them ourselves. You will quickly notice how easy it is to spot these thought patterns in others, and this can be one reason that working with an 'unreasonable friend' can be useful as they can work with you to spot these patterns and give you suggestions for how to question them appropriately.

Making changes and noticing thought patterns is a great way to start to pay attention to your thought patterns, and to make changes. Remember, the bigger your existing comfort zone, the more creative you'll have to get to find deliberate ways to step into your stretch zone.

Different types of change

Some of the changes I suggest are not 'forever' changes ... they're provocative! They're designed to provoke your thinking enough to push you into the stretch zone.

Provocative change

Often when we think about change, it's with the intention of doing it 'forever' in the new (changed) way, thus creating a new habit. Typically we want changes to show us a quick return on our investment either in terms of time or money. (If I learn a new skill, will I be able to charge more for my services, or I'll amaze my friends by 'rocking out' and playing the guitar). Provocative changes don't have to be forever changes – but they stimulate your thinking, and develop your awareness.

Provocative changes are not simply things 'to think about'. It is important that you carry out the activity, perhaps just one new activity per week. For example, one 'provocative' change would be to wear your watch on your opposite wrist, and the idea is that every time you look at your watch (which for most of us is an automatic habit) you're reminded that you're in the process of changing certain ways of thinking. It can be a prompt to remind you to adopt the growth mindset and to look for the opportunity. You don't have to wear your watch forever on your opposite wrist ... I would suggest at least a week though to get benefit, and then notice how it feels going back to the other wrist.

For more provocative change suggestions see -

raiseyourgame.biz/

It's also useful to remember that these provocative changes aren't one-off activities, as in order to grow, we have to continually experience our stretch zone. The more we grow, the more our comfort zone grows and the more thought we need to put into finding new ways to push ourselves and develop.

CHAPTER EIGHT

The secret life of positive emotions

"Happiness is not something ready-made. It comes from your own actions."

~ DALAI LAMA

Lifestyle changes

Depending on your perspective the changes detailed below might be described as big changes in attitude, or so trivial that they don't require a mention. However, they're included as they've been scientifically researched and the benefits have been proven. I use them with clients and have seen superb results. Whatever your starting point, either too big or too trivial, I encourage you to implement these changes because they will make a difference.

Positive Emotions

Relatively new research has shown the importance of positive emotions. Leading academic researcher on positive emotions, Barbara Fredrickson found:

"The leading scientific evidence tells us that positivity doesn't simply *reflect* success and health, it can also *produce* success and health."[22]

Positive emotions are not what happens after success is achieved – they're an important ingredient in creating success in the first place. Until relatively recently, there had been much research to establish the purpose of emotions such as fear, anger and sadness. However, relatively little research had taken place on the purpose of 'positive' emotions. Fredrickson's research changed all that, starting with her theory called "broaden and build". Essentially she discovered the purpose of positive emotions. They allow us to broaden our thinking around possible action and, to be more responsive to new ideas, and to build resilience. This is in contrast to 'negative' emotions, which seem to narrow our range of responses; think, of two responses to fear and anger: 'fight or flight'. So, to achieve transformational results you may want to embrace positive emotions to broaden your thinking and build resilience.

The evidence of the importance of positive emotions in health and well-being is overwhelming, you might find it surprising that there's not more media or governmental attention. Although, can you imagine if the government tried to mandate positive emotions alongside messages about healthy eating? The phrase "don't worry, be happy", a reggae classic may garner a more sinister Orwellian take if this were mandated by the government.

How much positive emotions

Research shows that in any 24-hour period it's extremely useful to have at least three positive emotions for every 'negative' emotion. There is also compelling research demonstrating that the highest performing teams, when working together have up to seven times as many positive emotions than negative emotions. Benefits accrue up to about eleven positive emotions for each negative emotion.

It's useful to remember that bad events typically have more impact than good events. Try this thought experiment, from Paul Rozin[23]:

Imagine a bowl of ripe red cherries. Just one cockroach amongst it would ruin the appeal. The impact of the one cockroach is significant. What about the other way round? Briefly think of a bowl of cockroaches, I doubt the addition of one cherry would make the cockroaches more appealing.

The strong impact of bad events, can mean that the good event can be overlooked.[24] In addition, to having a metaphor for understanding the impact of negative events, it also starts to inform how we might remember. Perhaps we have to pay more attention to positive events, and to selectively edit our memories,

It seems that most of us expect our memory to work like a DVD, making accurate recordings of all of our experiences. However, it's been shown this is not how memory works.[25] Professor Hood provides a useful metaphor of the store of memories of being like a compost heap, whilst most of the contents turn to mush relatively quickly, it is just the odd piece of content which retains its form, taking longer to decompose.

It's useful to say that ALL emotions have value. One key thing to remember is that **true** emotions tend to last for short periods of time. 'Negative' emotions are thought to have a short-term impact – fear provides the impetus for 'fight or flight' for example, and whilst there might be lingering effects of some of the stress hormones, the initial emotional surge passes quickly.

If 'something happens' and you seem to be still entangled in the mood hours or even days later, then it's probably not supporting you to get transformational results.

Of course, there are significant life events, like a death of someone very close that are likely to have accompanying moods, which can last (appropriately) for months, and I'm not suggesting that you short-cut yourself out of these. What I'm describing are the smaller events that might set you into a 'mood', which has a negative downward spiral on you and those around you.

"After my day, I have a right to be in a bad mood!"

You might be wondering what's so bad about being in a negative mood. Essentially it rubs off on all those around you. Moods both positive and negative go viral. You're grumpy to your team, and they're grumpy with the customer, who doesn't buy, buys less or subsequently tells his friend about the negative experience.

Perhaps you've had the converse experience whereby someone smiled at you at the checkout, and after the positive experience you found yourself smiling to the next person you met. Although we have what's sometimes described as a 'set point' for our habitual mood – this can be changed both positively and negatively by those around us. You intuitively know that some people give you a lift and boost your energy, and others seem to drain it – there's now research to support that emotions are contagious – we do seem to 'catch' them from those around us.

I suggest three things:

1. Increase your levels of positive emotions. It will mean you will feel better and experience life more positively, and it builds your resilience.

2. When you feel more positive you will be more likely to see opportunities – that shows we take in more information (broaden our thinking) and develop our ideas.

3. The third benefit is that it will have a knock-on effect on those around you. People enjoy spending time with positive people.

Starter kit for uplifting your mood

Many people languish in their bad mood. They don't have a plan to get out of it, and they don't do anything different.

Have a mood uplifting plan, and use it!

The first thing to recognise is that sometimes we all get stuck in a mood, snapping out of a mood is not always easy, and getting frustrated with yourself won't help.

The second step is to develop your 'mood lifting' plan. The best time to develop this plan is when you're feeling up-beat. I recommend it and it contains some of the following elements:

1. Stay calm, breathe more deeply (see below)

2. Develop and use your plan:

    ● *Listen to uplifting music*

    ● *Remind yourself of good times by looking at some photos*

    ● *Physical activity (e.g. a walk)*

3. Develop and use your sense of perspective

The third step is to use the plan when you notice yourself slipping into a bad mood – to help jump-start yourself into a better mood. If it's appropriate, then make the decision to JUMP right out of it into a positive mood.

Stay calm, breathe

Through my yoga practice, and having spent some time learning how to meditate, I've become increasingly aware of the importance of focused breathing. Over the years I've regularly practiced deep breathing as a way of calming down. The benefits from breathing were considered as a bit 'new age', until some research found how breathing affects the heart. A company called HeartMath developed a program of "controlled breathing and positive thinking" as a stress busting activity. What the yogis have known for several millennia now has 'science' to back it up.

Your breathing should be deep but not laboured – do what's appropriate for you. HeartMath suggest breathing out for a count of five and in for a count of five, and if that's too much for you, do less. HeartMath suggest focusing on a past enjoyable experience. I vary this with focusing just on breathing – on breathing in imagine the oxygen travelling down to your toes and circulating around your brain, and on breathing out, imagine exhaling the toxins. Find something that works for you.

Notice how you feel before you start; now give it a go.

Breathe in for a count of five, and out for a count of five. Do that for 90 seconds ... or nine full cycles – which I find easier than clock watching, and a gentle alarm works well too.

And breathe.

Notice how you feel now.

HeartMath suggest using their technique very regularly throughout the day.

Develop your plan

You probably already know what works for you.

- A play-list of music 'guaranteed' to raise your spirits.
- A selection of photos on your phone / computer that remind you of some great experiences.
- For most people 'doing' something is a guaranteed way to lift one's spirits – a walk or any form of physical activity is generally useful.

Sometimes people "phone a friend" who at the end of the conversation hasn't left them feeling any better. Whilst having a great social network to call on is important, check that those people you call do leave you feeling better, and check you're not over reliant on a single person in the group – and that you don't just call when you need your spirits lifted.

Vary what you use to uplift your mood

Develop your sense of perspective

Sometimes a particular event has contributed to your bad mood. If this is the case there can be different ways to gain perspective. Here are two of the most effective:

The perspective of time

It can be useful to keep what's happened in perspective. As you look at your vision, ask yourself if the event will matter in one year, five or ten years' time.

Perspective of importance

Close to where I live is a graveyard, and walking through the children's graveyard keep things in perspective for me.

One successful businessman I know carries a very small globe in his pocket, which reminds him of the size of the planet, and his contribution to the world.

Another well-travelled businessman asks himself if the problem he's experiencing is a 'first world' or a 'third world' problem. Inevitably as he is fed, clothed and has a roof over his head, it's a first world problem.

How to increase your daily dose of positive emotion

There are many ways you can, on a daily basis, get more positive emotion in your life. Take a moment to think about the things that bring a smile to *your* face, and the things that give you some form of positive emotion. You can include the jump for joy type of emotion, the types of things you might use to kick-start yourself out of a bad mood, as well as a sense of calm, contentedness, or a sense of peacefulness. These are still positive emotions, just the energy is different.

Some emotions are high energy, while some are low energy. The picture below shows positive and negative emotions and the level of energy associated with each.

The emotional quadrants

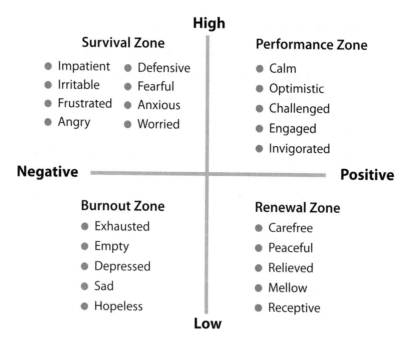

Figure 16 – *Energy of Emotions*
(T. SCHWARTZ, GOMES, & MCCARTHY, 2010)[26]

Schwartz, T., Gomes, J., & McCarthy, C. (2010). The way we're working isn't working : the four forgotten needs that energize great performance. London : Simon & Schuster.

Take five minutes to make a note of the things that you already know provide you with some form of positive emotion, whether high or low energy. You might find yourself thinking of things that have fallen off your radar, or you only do on holiday, perhaps long walks on the beach or a massage. You might contemplate things that you've never done that you would like to do, and you anticipate will have a positive affect on your life.

Your responses might include a film or a comedy that's pretty much guaranteed to leave you feeling uplifted. A piece of music that's upbeat or inspiring. A walk in nature, or even just watching the birds from your window.

Many people know what provides them with a high level of positive energy, and yet they don't actively make time to do these activities.

Ensure that you find time to put some of these activities in your diary. I'll describe more on how to find the time in Chapter 11.

What follows are a few more suggestions of proven things you can do to increase your daily amount of positive emotions.

- Gratitude / three good things
- Strengths
- Acts of kindness
- Time perspectives
- Savour

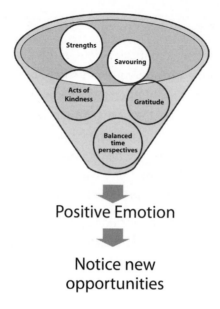

Positive Emotion

Notice new opportunities

Figure 17 – *Developing Positive Emotions*

Gratitude:

This is about being thankful. For some this may sound trite. Often in business there's a lot of busy-ness. With many 'to-dos' and projects to start, actions to take, and people to meet, work can sometimes be downright frustrating and our behaviours can become driven or obsessive. Sometimes in the rush to do the next thing we can lose sight of what we've done, what we've achieved and, more importantly, what we're thankful for. There's a whole heap of research out there that shows that a daily dose of gratitude is important for our well-being.[27] And exceptional well-being is important for achieving transformational results.

Find a way of acknowledging what you're grateful for in a way that suits you. Some people like to do this with their family over dinner. Other people use a daily personal gratitude journal where they record what they're grateful for. A clear cookie jar where you write your daily gratitude notes on with coloured pieces of paper can quickly become a visual reminder of the good in life – which can be especially helpful if you occasionally experience days when it just seems that nothing goes the way you'd planned – and not in a good way!

Acts of kindness

While many business people already have strong connections with charities, this is about finding opportunities to spread a little kindness, and not necessarily through formal giving to charity. Random acts of kindness will give you a warm feel good glow; however, it's important not to expect anything in return. It's been found that if you do several different acts of kindness in one day, it has a bigger impact than if 'kindness' becomes routine.

Different people 'give' in different ways. I don't want to prescribe what will work for you – experiment, and stretch your comfort zone. Suggestions include: pay a compliment, assist someone with their bags or a buggy, give *cash* to charity, volunteer your time to a charity or to a local community cause, and remember that acts of kindness don't have to be towards strangers, they can also be welcomed at home.[28]

Strengths

In a similar way to daily gratitude, you might also find it valuable to recognise daily the strengths that you used during the day. This can serve to build awareness of the broad range of strengths that you have, to develop them and finding new ways of using them. Ways to discover your strengths were covered in more detail in Chapter 4.

Change your time perspective

You probably intuitively know that people have different orientations to time. Perhaps you have the equivalent of an Aunty Nelly who harps back to the good old times, or an acquaintance, Bob who can find the cloud in every silver lining. Or perhaps you have a nephew who's always striving for his next goal. Each of the three people I describe has a different orientation to time.

Essentially there are four orientations to time: past positive, past negative, present and future. There has been some research around our time perspectives and how it affects us.[29] None of these time perspectives is right or wrong, although the research shows that having a balance of past positive, present, and future leads to higher levels of well-being. I mentioned earlier that higher levels of well-being and meaning of life are linked, and are more likely to lead to transformational results.

Past positive: Like Aunty Nelly, some people seem to look back with rose tinted glasses, remembering the good events, and pretty much ignoring what didn't go well.

You may also recognise people, like Bob, who have more of a ***past negative*** orientation to time – describing what went wrong in every situation and how awful it was.

Present: there are of course people who live in the here and now. There are different flavours of that, from small children who are very hedonistic and in the moment, through to a more *mindful*, considered and very aware approach.

There are additionally those people that are very goal and ***future orientated***.

Time travel

We can become fixed in or orientations to time, although with practice you can cycle through the different time perspectives. You've seen security monitors which show the input from different CCTV cameras around a site. The screen flips between images of one view of a car park to the next, then to a view of the entrance etc. You can adjust your time perspective almost this easily.

ACTIVITY Give it a go, and see just how easy it is to time travel. Think of a 'past positive' memory and enjoy it for a moment. Bring your awareness back to the here-and-now. For example, notice sensations in your left big toe, and then take a moment to focus on your vision. Great, it's as easy as that to switch time perspectives. Having this awareness of these different time perspectives will ensure that you can do this at will – if you find yourself stuck in a time perspective you can deliberately switch, although you don't need to do it as often as the CCTV security monitors!

Now that you've become aware of the time perspectives you will begin to notice that you and those around you have different default time perspectives. You may find that those people closest to you have similar time perspectives to you.

I think that one of the most unhelpful and insidious time perspectives is the past negative, and it can manifest itself in different ways. One of these ways is our habits of dramatic storytelling.

Stop dramatic storytelling

Sometimes people notice that they've built a reputation for storytelling ... "you'll never guess what happened next ..." and then detail the woes and misfortunes that befell them (often in a funny way). Even if this becomes a story on your way to achieving success, the impact on you can be negative, so I recommend you start to wean yourself off doing it. I've noticed that what people discuss develops a life of its own, and what you want to give life to is the positive, and growth aspects of you and your business.

Let's take a simplistic example of a couple who go on holiday for two weeks and overall, they have a great, although non-eventful time relaxing. The 'eventful' experience was arriving at the airport just in the nick of time to catch their flight. What do you think they describe on their return when talking with others? After the feelings of relaxation and the sun-tan has faded – what do you think is the first and key thing that is remembered and recounted about that particular holiday? It's typically not the bliss of gentle relaxation; it's the drama surrounding catching the flight. You don't need this drama in your life. Even if it happened – you don't need to recount the event again and again.

Some people object to a suggestion of selectively editing memories to deliberately include the good bits, although the above example shows how selective editing highlights the drama!

Ask yourself:

● When was the last time I told a story? When was the last time I exaggerated, even just a tiny bit?

Most of us don't realise we're telling stories, they are so ingrained. We're used to seeing drama unfold on TV in all areas from our News coverage to Soap Operas – and everything in between. Let's be clear that drama sells – and you don't have to live your life in a drama.

Sometimes storytelling patterns become further entrenched by the expectations of those around us. Friends are waiting to hear of your latest exploits ... poised waiting for the punchline. If you're looking for transformational results, stop storytelling, focus on your success and start to celebrate and share your accomplishments.

How to stop: Perhaps there's someone you can enlist to help you out. Generally people like to help – and often find it easy to point out a set of behaviours in others – so if you do notice you focus on the negative (perhaps through modesty for your success), you could ask someone around you to gently point it out. Agree with them in advance some options of how they could do it especially if you're mid-flow, and depending on the situation.

When people who smoke decide to quit, they are often encouraged to change their lifestyle for a couple of months to let their new healthy habits establish themselves. They're encouraged not to mix with their friends who smoke, just for a couple of months, and to think twice about visiting places where they've smoked in the past. Like someone who quitting smoking – it can be useful to acknowledge that you're changing a habit, and for a brief period of time, change your habits and patterns around meeting up with people who have old expectations of you. For example, if you're meeting business associates set a tight agenda – there will be less time for you to "take the stage". Alternatively use the time with them to find out more about them ... ask more questions – this could give you new information – perhaps raise your awareness of new opportunities.

Sometimes it's difficult, and even inappropriate to go 'cold turkey' on story telling. It can feel like you're supressing emotion. If you choose to share a negative story, do it deliberately and consciously recount events in a calm non-dramatic way. Search hard to find the positive, either in the event or in a different situation. Your negative emotion won't change the event, but over extended periods of time may negatively impact your health.

Creating a new past positive memory through savouring

Positive memories don't have to come from two weeks of holiday – they can be created from everyday events. Here's a three step process you can follow.

1. Do something

2. Slow down, deliberately notice the good, and your enjoyment

3. Relive it, either alone or with others

For example, yesterday seemed like an exceptionally warm spring day. I walked round the garden, noticing the new growth. I first sat on the grass, and then found myself lying back with the warmth of the sun on my face, the outline of our pear tree against the blue of the sky.

I'm writing this book today, looking at another lovely day; I have a choice as to how I feel. I could feel resentful at being 'stuck indoors', or to appreciate the choice I have to take time and write and to 'love doing what I'm doing' and to include a savouring experience, perhaps remembering the experience of yesterday before I find my flow and settle into my work.

Although this past positive sounds simple, it can be harder for 'go-getters' who are focused on their next result. Remember the purpose is to increase positive emotions, and these positive emotions build both your resilience and enable you to see useful connections and links from this broadened mindset, which is more expansive than the options seen through the lens of negative emotions.

Reliving a memory

Think about a favourite memory that you revisit from time to time. For example: "Do you remember when we won the business award? What a great night we had celebrating." Some people haven't collected as many of these past positive memories, or their memories have become somewhat tainted. That doesn't matter, you have new experiences every day – and you can deliberately choose to savour some of them, both during the event and after it.

Build your life like a photo album; it really is that easy! Choose the memories that make you smile, and decide to keep and revisit the positive ones. Storing memories is a bit like storing photos. I review the photos I've taken, and I want to put the photos that make me smile in albums.

As I upload the photos from the camera to the computer – there might be some photos I delete! I keep the best, and typically I delete the ones that I don't like. This may sound manipulative, and perhaps it is.

We do a form of editing our memories anyway; I think we may as well edit for the good, rather than the couple previously who edited their two weeks of bliss into a tale of near disaster. The benefit is that you'll feel good. When you feel good, as I mentioned earlier, the 'broaden and build' affect will kick in and you're more likely to be creative and innovative, seeing opportunities where previously you saw none.

It really is up to you. You can choose to keep cruddy memories, or you can create and enhance your memory album by revisiting and enjoying the events you want to. Focus on ways to develop your positive emotions.

Reliving a memory with others

 Many people think savouring has to be a solitary activity, when memories are actually enhanced by sharing – although it's really important to do this with someone who understands the goal of savouring.

 Find a buddy to savour with.

Not everyone is naturally good at savouring, and some people will insist on pointing out all the doom and gloom. Fortunately, people will let you know of their negative intentions by starting their response "yes, but ...", which, with practice, gives you ample time to put a smile on your face and make a conscious choice as to whether you 'join' them in their drama of doom and gloom, or whether you stay focused on the bigger purpose of savouring.

I'm not suggesting that you go into denial about flaws in events, and there's an appropriate time and place. In the same way that the Dreamer, Planner and Critic have their place in creating your vision, savouring should be done without your (or anyone else's) Critic.

You have a choice. It's like going to the fruit bowl. Sometimes you will want the juiciest plum, you have got the time to savour and enjoy the moist, sticky sweetness, and at other times, you'll want a 'no nonsense' banana that you can stuff into your bag and munch as you go. Choose what's appropriate for you; what you savour, and become discerning as to who you savour with.

Goal setting will be explored in Chapter 12, and having goals and working towards them is a form of developing a future time perspective. Developing your 'present' time perspective is, for most people, harder than it sounds.

What does it mean to 'stay present'?

Time, people, and technology are changing all around, and it's useful to 'stay present' to notice new ways and opportunities.

Have you ever found yourself listening to another person, your mind racing ahead, perhaps because you 'already know' the answer? When your mind is racing – either into the future or to the past, then you're not really being present. If you ever find yourself in one conversation thinking about what you're going to do next (whether that's next on the to-do list, next week or next year) or thinking about the past, then you're not really fully engaged with that person. Staying present is to listen with your full attention without pre-judging, either the person or the situation. With this level of awareness, fully engaged in the here and now it's more likely you'll pick up new nuances in what's being said. It can take some practice – so start now.

CHAPTER NINE

Shine a light on your fears

"Feel the fear and do it anyway."

~ SUSAN JEFFERS

Nothing that I've described so far requires any advanced skills, and yet if it was so easy, why hasn't every one taken steps to raise their game and achieve transformational results? For some it might be a lack of vision, for others it might simply be the lack of discipline of putting the steps into action. For many there can be something a bit deeper holding them back – fear.

Fears don't have to be 'big' to stop you in your tracks.

> One businessman I worked with would hesitate to introduce himself in business gatherings, and when he finally did introduce himself, he would underplay what he did as he was afraid of being seen as arrogant. In a networking environment it's hard to be passed referrals and opportunities if no one knows what he does! This fear of being seen as arrogant held him back.

Unexplored catastrophisation can accompany fears. Fears just have to be lurking in a dark corner of the brain, for them to begin to immobilise people. What I've found is that for most people, naming the fear and looking at it face on – seeing it for what it is rather than catching it out of the corner of an eye – is often enough to stop procrastinating and take action.

Most fears are not natural. Fear of loud noise is one of the exceptions, most other fears we've cultivated – probably unwittingly, and they've taken hold without our noticing.

Many people initially don't want to explore the original fear, for fear of what it might uncover. A friend describes this as the fear of looking under the rock.

"feel the fear and do it anyway" ~ **Susan Jeffers**

Sometimes the fear is more around how deep the fear might go. They become anxious that by exploring the fear it may uncover things 'best forgotten'. Often in these situations the fear of the fear is bigger and more destructive than the fear itself. Sometimes all it takes is to look at your fear face on, to decide to take some form of action. **Ask yourself**: what am I afraid of?

What's the worst that can happen?

Many people spend too much time thinking about what's the worst that can happen – they spend far more time catastrophising rather than creating compelling visions. Often their thoughts jump to this catastrophising without conscious awareness. I touched on this in Chapter 7 when I described some of the thinking patterns.

The antidote is to create your vision and take action.

If you notice that this is one of your habits (thinking about the worst possible outcome), then you might like to work out the exact chain of thoughts that leads you to that thought and calculate the probability that it will happen.[30] Also, calculate the 'best possible alternative', neither is accurate and it can be a way of providing an alternative to catastrophising.

What follows is a brief sample of some more common fears related to personal growth. These fears can be at the root of what's holding you back. Overcome these, and move forward in much larger steps.

Fear of loss of what you've already achieved

Fear of loss can come in two flavours: more tangible items of physical assets and material successes or the not so tangible assets of values, friends and lifestyle.

Many people keep the fear generalised.

It's useful to get specific.

Turn it from a vague fear to understanding specifically what the fear is so that you can either do something about it, or move through it to achieve transformational results. Work out what's fact, and what's a feeling or a hunch. Too often I've heard people complain that it's a "bad month" in business. Sometimes they deliberately do it so that they fit in with everyone around them, and more often than not, they're not in control of the situation or don't really know their performance indicators from their business.

If you find you have specific concerns, then you can address them head on, and act to mitigate these risks.

Fear of change

The status quo can be comfortable. I've said earlier that the world around is changing, and therefore if you're not changing and developing, you're essentially going backwards.

It's true that change will have knock-on effects – like a pebble being dropped into a still pond, there will be ripples that will last after the initial event. Can you be specific? What are you fearful that might change? Contrast it with the benefits of doing the same thing / staying the same?

Change can be uncertain, and we're not good at predicting what makes us happy.[31] For example, you probably think autonomy and choice is important to you; however, it's been shown that we can have too much choice, which, contrary to popular belief has been shown not to benefit us – this is described more fully in the section on fear of commitment.

Muddled thinking

 Many people have muddled thinking. Often we're not good at thinking things through thoroughly. We tend to have a bias approach, which gives large polarity and can seem to make things clearer; however, the risk is that it does not show the full picture.

 Many people spend too much time thinking and deliberating decisions without writing their thinking down, which often will expose flawed logic.

 When you have a decision to make, make notes – they will be clearer to review and will stop you going round in circles.

Here's an example of someone deciding to move office or to stay in the same location. First of all, they consider the disadvantages of decision A (e.g. not moving office), and the benefits of decision B (e.g. moving office). Within this framework, two key aspects are missed: the disadvantages of moving office and the advantages of staying in the same location.

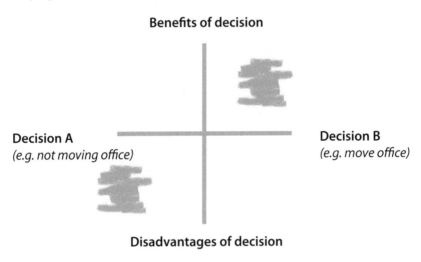

Benefits of decision

Decision A
(e.g. not moving office)

Decision B
(e.g. move office)

Disadvantages of decision

Figure 18 – *Showing Muddled Thinking*

I've seen many people thinking they were weighing up benefits and disadvantages, and have the polarity that I've shown above. Completing all the boxes can seem repetitive, as the words can sound similar; however, the nuances of the wording can be very informative. It might seem like it takes unnecessary time to write it down and, if the decision is important or has been going round and round in your head, then it can be well worth the few minutes taken to jot a few notes. It can also be useful to account for timescales. For example there may be short term disadvantages – the hassle of the move, reprinting of stationery etc., but these can be contrasted with long term benefits such as more space for the team.

So how do you make better choices

Write your thinking down. Rough notes work fine, they're for your eyes only. There's something about the process of writing that consolidates your thinking, plus you have the benefit of something to review so you don't go round and round.

1. Ensure you are clear what decision you're seeking to make.

2. Think things through in terms of costs / benefits for each – of the typically four quadrants.

3. The following four questions are designed to consciously scramble the conscious part of the brain to see if there's additional information held in your sub-conscious that would be useful to take into account. Don't worry if your answer is logically correct – it probably won't be – I recommend you DO note down your response. You may want to use a recording device, to capture exactly what you say. Answer the questions:

    ● *What would happen if you did (do X)?*

    ● *What would happen if you didn't (do X)?*

    ● *What wouldn't happen if you did (do X)?*

    ● *What wouldn't happen if you didn't (do X)?*

Another antidote to fearing change is to mix with different people. There are many ways to do this. Visit a different networking group, take a short class (whether tennis, photography, French), something that interests you and invokes your capacity for 'learning', and also gives you the opportunity to meet and mix with new people. More on this in the next chapter.

Fear or committing to a decision

In Chapter 1 I described the fallacy of keeping your options open; this can be made worse by fear of commitment. In a research experiment looking at choice, two groups of students took part in a photography course. They followed the same curriculum, which culminated in using a dark room to print three of their best pictures. At the end of the course the students were told that they would have to select one of their pictures to go for marking, and they wouldn't see it again. Here's where the two groups differed.

One group was told to make a decision 'there and then'; the picture would be sent away that evening 'for the records', and they would not get to see the photo again. The second group was also told to make a decision and, if they changed their mind over the weekend, they could swap it for one of their other pieces.

Would you prefer to have the choice to change your mind after a couple of days? Which group do you think was the most satisfied with their decision?

Most people think that having an element of choice to revisit the decision is useful. For example, we like to buy from shops where we can exchange the item if we're not fully satisfied – however, what the above and other research shows is that whilst we may like to have the choice, we're actually more satisfied when we "make the decision and move on". The group who made the irrevocable decision were happier. We have to make the decision and move on. Enter decisions with full commitment.

It seems that we have a certain number of decisions to make during the day, and it's been shown that these decisions require that same amount of processing whether a big decision or a small decision. It's almost like getting into your car, and no matter how far you're planning to travel, you're going to use a full tank of fuel. How do you plan to spend your 'decision making fuel', on the big decisions or the small ones?

Many people unwittingly waste their daily decision quota on small decisions. Because these take the same processing power as larger decisions – it's wasted energy.

 Create automatic processes that eliminate the need for small decisions – you can then spend your mental processing on the important decisions.

Fear of failure

> *"He who never made a mistake*
> *never made a discovery."*
>
> **~ SAMUEL SMILES**

"What if everything I've done was a fluke?" "What if I try to do it again and find I don't have the ability?" If you recognise that type of thought, then well done for recognising some of your thought patterns. Imposter syndrome as it is known is relatively common – so you're not alone. Secondly, here is what you can do about it.

Sure, there probably have been changes in environment that are different now to when you had your early successes, so it is a different route to navigate. Success typically isn't built on just *one* decision, so although one poor decision may take you off course – it's not likely to be catastrophic - especially if you're monitoring results, and are ready to make the next decision to make adjustments and improvements to your course. Even when things are going well you may want to make corrections to your course. An aircraft en route between airports typically heads directly for the destination runway less than 2% of the time. The rest of the time the plane is going in different directions, taking advantage of winds, avoiding no fly zones, and making continual adjustments in order to get where it's heading.

Interestingly, fear of failure can be entangled with low self-esteem, and low self-esteem can manifest itself as a fixed mindset. The need to be right aims to preserve one's self-esteem. Someone with a more fragile self-esteem or a fixed mindset is likely to see failure as destructive. Failure is not destructive, it's just feedback. Babies learning to walk, don't fall the first time and decide they've failed and give up with the decision "I'll never be a walker", having fallen, they get right back up again and give it another go. This willingness to get right back up again and give it another go is the trait of perseverance.

Many people don't deal with failure head-on; quite often and especially in times of high stress, they bury their head in the sand.

There is an expression: "There's no failure only feedback." 'Failure' becomes 'just' some information, and a requirement to do something different in the future.

With a growth mindset you'll be open to do things differently. Remembering that doing new things – or even old things differently – invokes learning. At times learning can be frustrating, which is why it's useful to have your vision. Your vision should be clear and compelling, and in Chapter 12 I'll discuss the importance of having a clear next step to keep you on track of achieving transformational results.

As described by the experiment in Chapter 1, failure may be represented as a door closing; in computer experiments with closing doors – the doors close forever. In life, however, new doors are opening all the time.

Fear of looking stupid

Have you ever feared doing or not doing something for fear of looking stupid? Perhaps there was a good opportunity – although because you noticed no one else was doing it – you feared looking stupid, and the fear was more compelling than taking a calculated risk. Some of this fear comes from the 'voices' inside your head, sometimes described as your inner critic.

Your inner critic can hold you to high standards, which can be really useful, and it can be disappointing when you don't meet them. Like the baby learning to walk, any new venture will have some faltering steps at the beginning. There may be some flailing around as we find our footing. If you judge yourself too harshly whilst flailing you'll never try anything new, because you won't meet your exacting standards in the timescales that you expect.

If you recognise fear of looking stupid, take a moment to consider the sort of situation or thing, which you would like to do, and is important to you, that causes you to think that you look stupid, or you fear looking stupid so you don't even attempt it?

Often we act differently with our friends when they make a mistake than we respond to ourselves. We're kind to them, or even when we joke it's with the intention of giving them a helping hand to get up, and get on with life. However, you might be harsh to yourself. Be kinder! Often mistakes happen because you're trying something new. So, when you're growing you're going to be making mistakes. It's part of the learning process. If you're not making mistakes; you're not growing.

Of course you may want to put some guidelines in place so that your mistakes are manageable, just in the same way you wouldn't encourage a friend who couldn't swim to jump into a reservoir to learn. If you're not used to making mistakes because of the fear of looking stupid, it can be useful to have some support and strategies in place to take things step by step, consider enlisting an 'unreasonable friend.' (See Chapter 14 for more info.) Rather than jumping in the reservoir, a strategy might be teaching your friend to swim in the relative safety of the local pool.

Depending on what events cause you to fear looking stupid will depend on the action you take. Here are some general suggestions that work.

You could learn something new, with people you've never met before; training courses are often a great place to learn. You can practice many skills, like 'speaking up' and 'asking questions.' With a group of new folk, this can lessen the embarrassment factor of making mistakes in front of your existing acquaintances. Of course once over the first hurdle, and you see the fear of looking stupid as one that doesn't have to hold you back, no doubt you'll be keen to make changes in different domains of your life.

Many people don't review and recognise the progress that they've made.

Celebrate effort, progress and achievements.

One benefit of a coach is to review successes as well as to develop and implement action plans.

Fear of uncertainty

Many people are creatures of habit, consistently doing the same types of things. People like routine; they feel comfortable. However, remember your 'comfort' does not equal your growth. In order to achieve transformational results you'll need to make some changes, and whenever you do anything new, there is an element of uncertainty.

Ask yourself:

● What is it about the uncertainty that causes me concern?

So what is the antidote? Develop your clear vision of the future. If there are different threads that you want to bring together – start to think about your ideal life – and how they are drawn together. Notice what's NOT in your vision – that can be an indication that it's time to let go of some things in your life. Consider whether you are you a consumer or a creator? Do you consume TV and newspapers, when you could be creating your future and enjoying transformational results?

Fear of disappointment

Often people don't get started because they fear that they will be disappointed, and at some level it won't really be what they want. Being clear on the outcome that you want, and thinking through some of the implications will ensure that it's not the equivalent of *King Midas*, asking for everything he touches to turn to gold. How will you know if your vision is well thought through? The truth is that you won't; you can do a good job of thinking something through and making a decision. A process for this is provided in Chapter 13.

Fear of regret

"Embrace the fear, leave regret for someone else."

~ SHÁÁ WASMUND

It's been suggested that decision makers in particular are prone to regret.[32] This is because people expect to have stronger emotional reactions to an outcome that is produced by action than to the same outcome when it is produced by in-action.

For example, in one interesting experiment saying 'yes' was associated with more regret than saying 'no' despite the wording of the question, which led to the same outcome. In a game of blackjack, players were asked either: do you wish to hit? Or, do you wish to stand? Researchers found that players who said 'yes' despite the question, experienced more regret than saying 'no' if the outcome was bad. It seems that our default response is 'no'. Saying 'yes' can cause feelings of regret.

This research has interesting implications for how you think about change. Consider that by not changing your business it *is* actually changing by stagnating, so in order to maintain the status quo you need to change. Back to the fruit bowl, you may not notice the signs of decay moment by moment, but in a time lapse sequence of photographs taken over days or weeks, you will clearly see the decay set in. **Ask yourself**: "Do I want the rot to set in to my business?" Take appropriate action.

You may have heard others caution you: "Don't do it, you might regret it." The emotion of regret is accompanied by feelings that "one should have known better".

Take calculated risks, know that there will be a likelihood of you experiencing regret when you deviate from the path of saying 'no' – but recognise you're overcoming natural instinct in order to achieve transformational results. My experience is, the more you move forward, the more decisions you take – the less time there is for regret.

Fear of success

Given you've already had success in your career, fear of success may not seem relevant to you. You already know what's needed to be successful. You've done it already – and often it's said that this is the hardest part. However, perhaps you weren't paying full attention to the steps you took to become successful, and therefore you fear doing it again or even the greater success it will bring.

I think it's a bit like learning to ride a bike – you may not fully remember how you learnt or be able to describe the laws of balance – and yet you can do it. Having learnt how to ride, you don't forget – perhaps there are a few initial wobbles after getting on a bike after even years out of the saddle – but the wobbles won't stop you.

Setting appropriate goal sizes can be useful. It's great to have a vision – and if it's been a while since you've been on a bike – whilst your goal may be to cycle the route of the Tour de France, you first might want to do a few shorter training routes before spending long days in the saddle. Indeed, perhaps the very first goal is to get the bike out of the shed, and check it's roadworthy, and then take a short exploratory cycle down the street and back.

Who can you bounce your ideas around with to see if your goals are challenging and yet achievable?

Harnessing different energies

There are two different energies involved in achieving transformational results. One is a strong energy that pulls you towards a goal or a vision. I call this 'towards' energy. You've begun to harness this by putting your vision in place.

There is also the energy of disgust or moving 'away from' the status quo, finding discomfort in your current way of being provides a surge of energy – much like a bucking bronco. This 'away from' energy is forceful and doesn't have a clear direction. So, you've got your vision, you've set your course; it's time to harness the power of the 'away from' to really accelerate things.

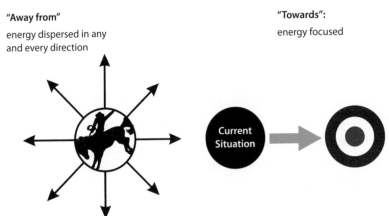

"Away from"

energy dispersed in any
and every direction

"Towards":

energy focused

Figure 19 – *Energy of "Away From" and "Towards"*

Here's an activity designed to find your 'away from' thinking, and harness some powerful energy.

Most feared obituary

The most feared obituary is based on living a long life without any positive changes in your current standards, priorities and goals.

Pretend that you have failed to change unhealthy and unhappy patterns that you have now and project how these problems will get worse as you get older and die. In fact, any small problems that you currently experience can be expected to get much worse over the many years that you 'let yourself go', deteriorate and do nothing to make changes to your life in any way.

Next, pretend that you have agreed to write your own obituary just before you die. This is a very personal and detailed obituary for all of your friends and family to see.

If your original vision was only mildly compelling, this activity should have provided a surge of 'away from' energy. There can be the realisation that staying the same is not an option. With your vision you have a direction – and this activity can provide the surge of energy to overcome inertia to start you moving. Moving from stationary takes the most energy. This activity done properly will provide that initial burst of energy to propel you forward – either to work on refining your vision or making strong steps to make it happen.

Before I describe how to develop specific goals based on your vision, I'd like to describe the importance of continuing your professional development.

CHAPTER TEN

Expanding your horizons

"The real voyage of discovery does not consist of seeking new landscapes, but in having new eyes."

~ MARCEL PROUST

Personal Development

I've alluded to the fact that it's essential to continue to develop your skills, specifically from the perspective of developing a growth mindset, and this is just one way of getting quality new stimulus. In order to have new ideas, and to develop new ways of thinking, it's useful to have new stimulus.

This chapter explores how you can find new stimulus. You will notice that some of the ideas overlap. They're listed separately to give you the broadest range possible in order to deliver transformational results. You can do some or all. Your criteria for deciding will depend on a number of factors; how much time you have available, how quickly you want to achieve transformational results as well as the type of activities that you might enjoy.

Figure 20 – *Sources of New Stimulus*

Meeting and talking with new people

There are lots of interesting and stimulating people around – you just have to find them, or find ways to find the interesting nuggets. Ideally you're looking for people who don't share the same views as yours – which will gently challenge your thinking and provide food for thought and, more importantly, will fuel your growth. However, not everyone you meet will be able to provide you with useful challenges to your thinking (see Chapter 6 on values), and of course meeting the right people can take time.

Who do you spend time with?

It's been suggested that who you spend your time with will influence your income to within 5%. Ask yourself: who do I spend time with that influences me? Our natural response is to 'fit in', especially with our long established networks, which may not encourage new thinking. You may find existing networks don't want you to change – you may find they give subtle signals for you "not to get too big for your boots".

Take a look at where you spend your time, and who you spend it with. Ask yourself how your brain is getting the new stimulus it needs to take your thinking to the next level. Of course you're not going to change your employees – but what about your stimulating friends? Are you spending enough time with them? Do you need someone to challenge you? And of course there are 'virtual mentors' found in the pages of books and audio CDs. If you already spend time in the car – then at least occasionally you could listen to a stimulating audio book instead of the radio. Or perhaps you need to be proactive and meet new people locally.

Networking groups

The business owner has access to many groups if they so wish. You may have to be discerning in where you look for this stimulation, although all stimulation can be useful with a growth mindset.

There are many business networking groups; an internet search of networking groups or events in your area will find some. These groups vary enormously in their format and style and therefore the type of people they attract – so even if you've tried it in the past and didn't find it useful – find a different group. If you find attending these groups uncomfortable – excellent, you're stepping outside of your comfort zone.

Business Coach

A business coach can be a great investment and should be able to provide you with a high quality challenge on a weekly basis, which is a highly effective way to get new and high quality stimulus. I'll talk more about different types of support including informal buddies, mentors and business coaches and coaches in Chapter 14.

Do new things

Doing new things begins to program the brain for change; it sends the message that you're up for doing things differently, especially if you're also programming your brain to constantly look for opportunities for growth. Doing new things can provide the added benefit of meeting new people – although not necessarily. You might take up a solo activity like running, editing your photos on the computer or simply visiting a new location. The benefit is twofold. You get a mental rest from your day-to-day activities as well as some new mental stimulus.

You might find yourself applying insights from one activity to another. For example, the anglepoise lamp was created by applying the jointing principles found in the human arm. [33]

Playing scrabble one Christmas really demonstrated to me the importance of having high expectations. I'm not a keen Scrabble® player. However I was browsing through the 'rule book', and I read something about getting scores of 25 – such scores were not on my radar. In that instant I found that fact quite amazing. I'd always just been pleased to find a word – scores of 25 seemed high, and caused me to challenge my expectations. Very quickly I started looking for ways to score 'more'. I started to see the game of scrabble less in terms of a word game – rather I began to see it as a game of getting a high return on investment. I started to take decisions as to what would start to form acceptable returns on my investment of letters.

In addition to playing a game and getting some relaxing down time, I learnt two lessons; a simple one about return on investment, and a significant one about expectations. If our expectations are low, then we are satisfied with low results.

Sometimes you won't see that you're held back by your own expectations, or the expectations of others. You're too immersed in the existing culture to notice that there is another way. You have to find a way to get out of your current culture, in order to change your expectation. What follows are some suggestions as to how to do this.

Enrol on a short course

Find a subject that you're interested in and find a short course. Find something that you at least think you will enjoy (rather than something that would be "good for me to do").

It doesn't matter on the subject matter, it could be related to your professional development, or it could be for pure indulgence. When you created your vision, perhaps there was an activity that you'd always wanted to start, or improve ... this could be the opportunity.

It can be useful to think and write a few notes about why you're signing up for the course, what you hope to get out of it, and how long you're going to commit to doing it. As I described in Chapter 2, if the course involves learning a new skill, sometimes in the middle it can look and feel like failure. To help yourself through this patch, as you select your course take five minutes and write down the reasons you've chosen it. Having clear written reasons describing your original drivers and motivations can help with your motivation to continue when facing the bit in the middle. It doesn't matter if there's a qualification (or not) at the end of it. In some ways aiming for a qualification can keep you motivated; the main purpose of this is to mix with different people, and get new stimulus in order to raise your game.

Learn new skills

If you lead people – being a beginner again can be a useful reminder of some of the growing pains that beginners experience when they learn new skills. When you've done something for years it just seems obvious. Find something (an activity, a language, an instrument, a subject) that you're interested in, and are also a relative beginner in. Actively engaging in this skill can be a good way to experience the learning process, the stages from unconscious incompetence and the feelings of frustration commonly associated with conscious incompetence. The goal isn't necessarily to get to develop your skills to the level of unconscious competence. You will have a rich source of new information, which will provide you with reminders and opportunities to find a new way to handle setbacks, and the ability to notice what happens to your emotions. With that awareness you can develop your empathy towards the people you lead around their learning and development, as well as reinforcing your own store cupboard of skills.

Playing games

People approach games as they approach life. Whether golf, cards, chess or some other activity, how do you play games? Do you play to win? Do you do it for the sheer fun, to escape? More importantly when you start to play, can you stay in the game, and are you open to learning or do you withdraw?

I'm not suggesting that you invest hours in playing games, your time is precious and if you do play games, notice your responses and be open to the learnings.

Personal Development

Smaller businesses are typically very bad at investing in training for either themselves or their team. [34] And when investment does happen, it's likely to be around technical skills. Often traditional 'personal development' is seen as a peripheral skill – something that's 'nice to have' although because not core to your business's success, these skills get left out in favour of more technical skills. As I mentioned in Chapter 7, often business is started by the type of person Gerber describes as a Technician. Often the skills that need developing are those of Manager and Entrepreneur. Developing as an entrepreneur requires you to communicate with an increasing range of diverse people, on a range of topics.

However, there's good news; there are a broader set of skills that are universally important, and learnable. As you consider raising your game a first step can be to appraise your current skill level. Whilst this book can't provide feedback (unbiased or otherwise), what it can do is provide you with some new stimulus and provide different ways of thinking. These skills can be transformational.

The types of skills I'm talking about are:

- asking questions
- listening
- building rapport
- discipline

Sure everyone can ask any old question, and we all think we listen; however, as you continue on your journey to transformational results, these are just two of the skills which will typically benefit from you spending time refreshing.

How to improve your questions

I've noticed that most people ask questions, often without really thinking, and certainly without a systematic approach hoping to get a great solution.

Einstein is quoted as having said that if he had one hour to save the world "*he would spend fifty-five minutes defining the problem and only five minutes finding the solution*". The power of the answer lies in the power of the question. Let me explain what I mean. Since our childhood, we have been trained to "answer the question", and typically when asked questions – that's what we do – we answer them. We get slightly habitual in our question asking – and no surprise that people's answers become slightly habitual.

What happens if you ask a different question? Often it can seem that people clam up: often they don't respond instantly. What's often happening is that they're thinking about things in a new way before responding. Brilliant. This is the time to pause, not to jump in and ask a different question. Your question had impact – let the question take effect, their answer may not be the 'top of the head' version that you're expecting – it might be slower and less thought through – and you've discovered a deeper level of answer. Of course you have to listen to the new answer and respond, perhaps with another question to dig deeper, but for the moment let's stay with the structure of questions.

You might think that what follows is just 'semantics', and playing with words. Let's explore some examples, remembering that people are very good at answering the question that's presented.

"Is there a problem?"

This is closed questions (i.e. one that elicits a yes or no answer). Closed questions have their place. Often closed questions close down thinking; they lack direction or purpose. They can be useful to confirm facts, and at the end of a conversation to close down thinking and confirm commitments and actions. Closed questions do nothing to *open* the thinking, or engage the brain of the other person.

Many people get too relaxed with their questions and ask closed questions. Other people often do answer with more than yes or no (we've been trained to as children), however, responses are based on what information is easy to provide / or they want to provide, rather than engendering new thinking.

Develop your question asking skills and reap the benefits of harnessing the benefits of both brains engaged in the conversation – ideal longer term if you want to be able to delegate.

So the alternative is the open question:

"What's the problem?"

Both parties are now focused on the problem. The question will elicit more information about the problem. There are other open questions:

"Why is there a problem?" or "What's caused the problem?"

These questions start to draw attention to the causes of the problem. This can be useful if the process will change as a result of the discussion, *however*, 'why' questions can cause defensiveness. Depending on the time in relation to the problem and the defensive nature of the people involved in the discussion, the question may be heard as "who caused the problem" – and involve an exercise in finding who to blame. Blame typically doesn't fix problems; it just causes people to become closed and defensive.

Aesop Fable of the Sun and the Wind

The North Wind boasted of great strength. The Sun suggested there was great power in gentleness.

Spotting a man travelling on the road, they set a challenge to see which one could remove the coat from the man's back the quickest.

The wind began. He blew strong gusts of air, so strong that the man could barely walk against them. But the man clutched his coat tight against him. The wind blew harder and longer, and the harder the wind blew, the tighter the man held his coat against him. The wind blew until he was exhausted, but he could not remove the coat from the man's back.

It was now the sun's turn. He gently sent his beams upon the traveller. The sun did very little, but quietly shone upon his head and back until the man became so warm that he took off his coat and headed for the nearest shade tree.

Change the focus from obstacle to solution

What happens if, instead of focusing on the problem or obstacle, the focus becomes the solution? For example:

"How are we going to fix this?"

"What will it take for us to find a way round this obstacle?"

"What's the quickest way for us to solve this?"

"What would be an innovative solution to this problem?"

And when there is a problem – it can be very useful to have two brains focused on how to solve it.

I / We / You

Of course most people don't like the use of the 'we' when you mean you, so if it is up to the other person to fix, then it can be more honest, and provide clarity to be explicit. Another option is to 'take the people out' of the conversation. "How will this get fixed?" This can be especially useful if it's an area of contention.

Problem focus

It's still interesting that in the above set of questions there is still significant focus on the problem. Traditional approaches ask about problems, which seek to find what causes problems in order to eliminate, reduce or overcome problems. There's a different school of thought called Appreciative Inquiry (AI).[35]

Appreciative Inquiry

Appreciative Inquiry (AI), which focuses entirely on what goes well. It's an approach that focuses on the exceptional and good moments, and then designs the organisational processes to maximise the likelihood of that happening on a consistent basis. AI uncovers new thinking by asking a different set of questions (see figure 19). For example: when we deliver excellence – what is that? How do we deliver excellence every day?

Al is a strengths based approach, which recognises that often people do a great job. There are always positive exceptions and so the AI approach explores what has to happen for these exceptions to be designed into the processes in order to become the norm. Of course AI is a particular approach, which is effective for workshops, brainstorming sessions or any situations where you particularly want new thinking.

Typically AI is an activity in which the whole organisation participates.   This gives buy in to create the organisation's transformational results.

Appreciative Inquiry: Overview

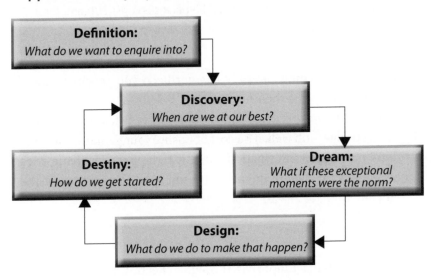

Figure 21 – *Appreciative Inquiry*

Listening

Enhance your listening so that you can listen for new opportunities. Especially with your new questioning skills you'll be digging a deeper mine, and finding a whole heap of new information – if you're listening out for it.

You know that hearing is different to listening. You too get frustrated when people say 'yes', when they think they heard, or you find yourself mis-quoted. They haven't actually listened to what you've said. Perhaps the nuance has been missed.

One of the best things you can do for another human being is to give them a "damn good listening to".

> As a coach, listening is an important aspect of the work I do, and I'm often surprised at how impactful it can be. I've worked with clients where the first session has been the 'unloading' of information and feelings, after which they feel much better and less likely to 'quit'. "I now realise I can do this stuff," one client said. Another commented after one of their first sessions: "I dreamt for the first time in a long time, I'm now sleeping properly."

Of course if listening carefully has not been your normal way of being with people – then not just you, but those on the receiving end may at first experience your new attentive listening behaviour as a bit strange – oh well, it's a cost of raising your game and seeking to find new bits of information. Do it with rapport, be gentle – it's not a quiz show where the other person is on the spot to get the 'right' answer.

Reflecting back

One way to build rapport is through reflecting back. People do business with people they get on with. One way to build rapport is through your ability to reflect back. Listening is great – and you probably have heard much of what's been said – the question becomes: how does the other person know that they've been heard?

The skill is in the reflecting back what they said, which lets them know that they have been heard. Again it sounds simple, and yet it is very powerful.

Prefix

You don't have to agree with another person to let them know that they've been heard.

You can prefix what you think you heard with phrases like:

"it sounds like ..."
"it seems that ..."
"I think I heard you say ..."

Words are important

Let's say I said the following ...

"I enjoy riding my bicycle. From my home I can cycle in local woods, along country lanes and unmade roads and bridleways. I love the fresh air, being out and about."

How would you reflect back?

"Sounds like you enjoy riding your bicycle?"
"It seems like you love the fresh air?"
"I think I heard you say you can cycle in local woods without requiring additional transport to get there?"

The above are accurate reflections. There are of course other things that you might accurately reflect back.

However, what about the following?

"you enjoy mountain biking"
"you enjoy exercise"
"you enjoy being in the countryside"

These may be true, and they're not an accurate reflection of what's been said. The speaker is being told what they like. There are two problems with this; firstly, it may not be an accurate reflection of what's been said. Secondly, how much do you like being told something? Most adults resist being told.

Many people are sometimes concerned that, by not adding an interpretation to what's been said, a clear and simple reflection sounds too stupid. The risk is that it 'jars' with the other person. Their interpretation can sometimes be inaccurate – and skips steps in building rapport.

Accurately reflect the words that are used.

Don't take my word for it – find a willing friend and practice. Have them talk – just for a minute or so perhaps about a hobby, and then you reflect back (you could separately reflect back the words they use and then see what happens when you include an interpretation). The important thing is to notice both their verbal and their non-verbal responses. Do they respond "yea, sort of" as you reflect back … or do you notice a nod of the head and a crisp and clear "yes, yes, that's it".

"Yea, sort of", often means they're too polite to say "no" – they can see the link that you've made, and are being generous in their response. If you have a friend or acquaintance, who can be precise or pedantic in their responses – then they are the ideal person for you to practice this skill with. As a matter of course they automatically will give you feedback on the accuracy of your listening and reflecting back.

New questions will start to elicit new information and, by developing your listening skills, you will be 'tuned in' to hear the information. The ability to accurately reflect what's been said builds rapport with the person you're speaking with, which can be handy, especially if you're asking different questions, which start to have them think differently and cause their brain to ache!

Having access to a new quality of information, a new view on life are useful tools on your journey to achieving transformational results. How do you get feedback and pointers to take your skills to the next level? Athletes have coaches to provide them with feedback and to provide discipline when spirits are low.

Many people think "I should know this stuff", and they don't invest in themselves to develop skills and grow.

Be willing to trip up occasionally, to learn from your mistakes and ultimately to grow. You don't have to do it alone.

Ask yourself: when was the last time that I invested in myself? Would I benefit from more investment, or just someone to bounce ideas around with? Chapter 14 will describe how coaching can support you.

CHAPTER ELEVEN

Time mastery

"Do not squander time, for that's the stuff life is made of."

~ BENJAMIN FRANKLIN

Even if everyone has the ability to raise their game, not everyone has the time. Finding or making the time takes discipline and a ruthless approach to what your priorities are and what you can stop doing. However, you have bought this book so you are motivated. The first step is finding out where you spend your time currently.

ACTIVITY

If you really don't know where you spend your time, you may have to invest some time in accurately monitoring your time usage. Create or download a table showing different time slots in 30-minute segments and as you go through the day, make a *brief* note of how you spend your time. Do this for a couple of days to get an idea of how you spend your time. You will begin to see what takes your time. Blank forms are available on **raiseyourgame.biz**/downloads

06:00 – 06:30	
06:30 – 07:00	
07:00 – 07:30	
07:30 – 08:00	
08:00 – 08:30	
08:30 – 09:00	
09:00 – 09:30	
09:30 – 10:00	
10:00 – 10:30	
10:30 – 11:00	
11:00 – 11:30	
11:30 – 12:00	
12:00 – 12:30	
12:30 – 13:00	
13:00 – 13:30	
13:30 – 14:00	
14:00 – 14:30	
14:30 – 15:00	
15:00 – 15:30	
15:30 – 16:00	
16:00 – 16:30	
16:30 – 17:00	
17:00 – 17:30	
17:30 – 18:00	
18:00 – 18:30	
18:30 – 19:00	
19:00 – 19:30	
19:30 – 20:00	
20:00 – 20:30	
20:30 – 21:00	
21:00 – 21:30	
21:30 – 22:00	
22:00 – 22:30	
22:30 – 23:00	
23:00 – 23:30	

Many people leave the tracking until the end of the day.
They then try to remember what took their time, which can be
time consuming and miss some of the nuances of interruptions
and other miscellanea that happens and is useful to track.

Make a note of what takes your time as it happens.
You will easily start to see what takes your time.

You may find that by simply doing the above activity you become slightly more efficient. However, now you need to look at the activities that you're spending your time on, compared to your priorities.   When you've established where the discrepancy is, you can make changes, which will give you more time to achieve transformational results.

Stephen Covey suggested there are different categories of time usage. He suggested two criteria for listing activities – urgency and importance.[36]

Many people only prioritise by urgency, and never stand back
to consider their priorities and what's important.

Having a vision will help you to know what's important
to you. Knowing what's important will help you
to prioritise.

Urgent/Important

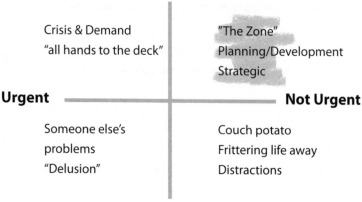

High importance

Crisis & Demand
"all hands to the deck"

"The Zone"
Planning/Development
Strategic

Urgent ———————————————— **Not Urgent**

Someone else's
problems
"Delusion"

Couch potato
Frittering life away
Distractions

Low importance

Figure 22 – Urgent and Important

OK, in terms of prioritisation and making good use of the time you have, you're aiming to get more time in the quadrant in the top right: The Zone ... doing activities of strategic importance ... first let's take a look at activities in other quadrants that get in the way, slow you down and make you less efficient.

Not urgent not important

Firstly, there are things that you spend your valuable time doing, which are **not urgent and not important**. It's the times in your life where you find yourself as a couch potato sitting zombified in front of the telly. It's not the active enjoyment of TV – enjoying your favourite TV show, or relaxing in front of a good movie. This is a mindless place, a place of either distraction or frittering (your life away).

Ask yourself:

● what do I think I do that might be described in this way?

If there are things that you regularly do in the not urgent not important – this is the first place you can stop doing things. Perhaps mindlessly watching TV, or diligently responding to ALL your email fits in this category. More tips will follow.

Urgent but not important

The next category of activities, are those which are **urgent and not important.** A clear distinction to make here is that it's not important TO YOU. Often urgent but not important activities involve other people and *their* priorities. Sometimes it can be other people's emergencies, and it can simply be a ringing phone that you drop everything to answer when you don't even know who's on the line. A ringing phone can be hard to ignore in the same way as someone standing in the doorway.

Don't be deluded into thinking that their priority is yours, or that being busy in this quadrant means you are moving your business forward. Sure, it's nice to be wanted, and it's often easier to be swept along by someone else rather than taking a step back and making an active choice *not* to do something and risk a minor confrontation. Of course, as with all roles the items in this category will vary by role. Helpdesk staff waits for the ringing phone – and that is their job.

Choices here can also be because of our internal 'rules', for example, that we should answer every email. However, activities you undertake in this quadrant are not taking you towards your goals. In a moment I'll suggest you look at your time audit, to see how seduced you get by other people's priorities.

Many people are swept along by this 'delusion' prioritising items in the urgent and not important category even though it's not important to them.

 Know your priorities and be ruthless with time but gracious with people.

It can be hard to change the expectations of others, especially if in the past you've always been especially helpful – this is why you will need to be very clear what your priorities are.

Taking on other people's problems

 Business owners tend to take ownership of almost all of the problems in the business. This can make delegating a challenge.

This is not surprising because as a business owner the buck stops with you. ***But*** every time you take the problem away from one of your team, you inadvertently dis-empower people, and open yourself up to interruptions and queries. Changing your way of thinking can support you to support your team. This change won't happen overnight. Ask questions, ask them what they are planning to do, or would do if you weren't there. Encourage them to think more broadly, and take responsibility. When you empower one of the team with resolving a problem, you will want to be sure they have both the skills and motivation to fix it. This will probably mean that you need to develop your questioning skills, and have a solid process for following up – after all, you're not abdicating responsibility, you're simply delegating.

Your beliefs and mindset are especially important here, because if you believe you cannot trust others to make decisions or do work to the quality you would expect, then you may have some work to do on your mindset. Perhaps you don't have the right team in place, and you'll still need to work on your mindset to ensure that you're attracting the right people; for example, are you paying enough?

Urgent and important

Tasks that are both **urgent and important** are the metaphorical FIRES that have to be put out! These are the critical situations that have to be prioritised, that you drop everything for. This is where you're in DEMAND. For many people this creates a bit of an adrenaline buzz – and whilst it's demanding – it's also responding rather than being proactive. Sadly many people are in the habit of leaving things until they are both urgent and important and simply *have* to be done.

It's often said that if people like crises, putting out fires, and the ensuing glory, then they can be good arsonists leaving things until they become urgent, adding a bit of drama and excitement to the day. If you notice this is a pattern, you can also ask if you get some sort of pay-off by being the fixer and saving the day. It might be the drama in telling the story ... "you'll never guess what happened today ..." or it might simply be the adrenalin buzz of being in demand. What work culture have you created? What behaviour is rewarded? Saving the day, or the focus on prevention?

Over the long term, the goal would be to reduce the number of actions or activities that reach this category so that you have time to be proactive, and more strategic. The drama might disappear from your days; you might find your repertoire of new stories where you "save the day" dwindles, and this energy that you spend on "saving the day" and story-telling can be put to better use, in developing your strategy to create transformational results.

Not urgent and yet important

Finally, we get to THE ZONE. This is where you're aiming to spend more time. Strategy, planning and prevention activities tend to be the items that are categorised in important but not urgent. This tends to range from focus on health to business strategies. No one tends to shout at you for not having your strategy in place (or going to the gym) – these are typically not urgent – so you have to have the discipline to put focus on it, and to prioritise it.

Anything to do with planning / strategy / health (until it becomes a crisis!), fits in here.

How to find more time!

Of course there are just 24 hours in a day. We each have access to the same number of hours, so it's how we use them that make the difference. The goal is to make THE ZONE bigger, to do more strategic work. Most people don't have the time to do make this switch immediately, so it's about starting in a different quadrant. Whilst it might be ideal to reduce the number of crises that you deal with – typically that can't be changed overnight either. **Urgent and important** emergencies will continue to happen, at least until you've put some systems in place to enable others to deal with some of these priorities, perhaps through writing systems or scripts. So, where can you get more time?

Review your time audit

First, take a look at how you've been spending time currently. Grab several highlighter pens, and give each of the four categories a different colour, and take no more than five minutes to review how you spend your time and highlight the type of activity you're spending your time doing.

When you look at how you spend your time, no doubt there will be a range of activities across all four categories. There's no perfect balance, it depends on the type of activities you're involved in. There are some useful questions that you can **ask yourself**: what do I notice about where I spend my time? How productive am I? What could I do to become more productive?

If you fritter away your time in 'couch potato' i.e. **not urgent and not important** (DISTRACTION) it can be as a result of spending too much time dealing with constant crises in **urgent and important**. It's not good quality downtime – but it's necessary for mental recovery from all those high adrenaline fire fighting tasks.

The place to gain time in the short term is to be more disciplined with **urgent and not important.**

Put the 'big stuff', your priorities or rocks in your diary first.

What are your rocks?

You may have come across a similar story of a professor speaking on time management. He pulls out a large glass jar, and carefully fills it with large stones about the size of tennis balls. He asks his students if the jar is full, and certainly there's no room for any more large stones. He pulls out a bag of smaller pebbles and gently pours them in, allowing them to fall between the large gaps between the stones. Once again he asks his students if the jar is full. He carefully takes some sand and pours it into the jar. The sand fills the gaps between pebbles and stones, but this time when asked, the students hesitate when asked if the jar is full. The professor finally pours in water and fills the jar.

The point of the story is to ensure that the big rocks, the things that are important to you, make it into your schedule first. Other things will fit round the rocks, but if you fill your diary with 'trivia' first, then there's no space for the important stuff.

The first thing to do is to prioritise what's important to you, and to stay focused on it, so that when you get interruptions you can prioritise appropriately. In the same way that you've created a personal vision, if you haven't already created one for your business – it can be useful to keep you focused. Here are some other common timewasters with suggestions:

EMAIL with its constant pop-up boxes notifying of new mail often seems important – is it really? ... could it wait a couple of hours if you checked at set points during the day?

How can you reset expectations about how quickly you respond? If it's appropriate, you can set email to manually 'sync' a couple of times per day. What about newsletters? Can you declutter your main email account?

Twitter is a great tool and can also be a distraction. If there are key people you want to follow, you can create lists, and stay up-to-date without having a constant stream of tweets.

Phone calls? Does your phone have to be on 24X7? Often people are more effective if they have a set time to receive / make calls. How do you handle interruptions? How can you quickly ascertain the importance of the interruption, remember to be gentle with the person, and ruthless with time.

Remember you have a certain amount of 'decision making fuel' (Chapter 9); use it wisely.

What activities can you stop?

For any task there are a limited set of possible choices. Although many activities will still need to get done, there are some which only you can do – for example, you can't send someone to the gym on your behalf!

Does it need to be done?

- Stop

Can someone else do it?

- Delegate
- Outsource

If you really have to do it, can you?

- Plan / defer / slip
- Speed up

Stop!

Sometimes prioritisation can include stopping some activities. You might decide to stop some things that don't add value to your life. Sometimes there are no implications to stopping an activity.

For example, I haven't watched more than about an hour of TV a week for several years. Sure, there are some conversations about the latest TV drama that I don't engage with, but overall I haven't noticed a negative impact.

Short-term stop

There may be some things you can stop in the short term, for a limited duration of a couple of weeks, or even months, which will gain you more time. This might be enough to create and develop plans which will be effective longer term.

- Let your friends know you're working on a project, which is taking time for the next couple of weeks. Put a date in the diary to meet up and celebrate at the end (this will also give you a deadline to work towards).
- Save time by having the supermarket deliver your shopping.
- Only check personal email once per day, and perhaps respond in a batch even less frequently.
- No newspapers, no TV, and no radio.

Do you need to do it?

Perhaps there are activities that still need to get done, whether at home or in the office, but do YOU need to do them? Is there someone in the team who could do it, or does it need to go external for someone else to do the 'whole job'.

Outsource

Business woman Sháá Wassmund, founder of Smarta.com described her number one business tip as "get a cleaner".

Some 'whole jobs' can be outsourced: from mundane home chores such as ironing, cleaning or mowing the lawn, through to business functions such as HR and legal advice.

Could someone else do a reasonable job of tending to the tasks that you don't have time for. Find someone locally to outsource your tasks. You may find that you initially baulk at the cost; however, if time is your most important resource and you can't find the time from stopping other activities – even on a short term basis – then just do it.

How much is your time worth? How much time do you spend doing these things? How much time would you save by having someone else do them? Compare how valuable your time is compared to how much it costs to pay someone else to do these tasks?

Delegate

Much delegation starts with the well-intentioned words "can you just …"; however, often the team member doesn't get the appropriate training on how to do the task. On a good day this 'non-training' works just fine; however, when the resultant output from the task doesn't meet expectations, it's too easy to give up on delegation, and think you have to do everything yourself. This is often in part due to you not sharing your expectations of what the end result will look like. Effective and long-term delegation may involve writing the process. This is beneficial to ensure that: there's clarity on what the completed task looks like, there are appropriate 'checks and balances' to ensure that things don't fall through the net, and so that anyone can do the task. Up front this can take a little time. Even if not the whole task can be delegated – you may find there are aspects that someone else can do.

If the task needs to be done by you, does it need to be done now, or can you plan it for another time, perhaps to action in batches for greater efficiency. Alternatively you may find there are quicker ways of doing things.

Go faster

Some activities can be done faster with no loss of impact. How productive are your meetings? What would happen, rather than sitting, if everyone were to stand? What would happen if your meetings had a clear structure and everyone was clear on the decision making process?

Perhaps you have to read a newspaper or journals to stay up to date with news from your business; how long does it take? Could you do it faster? What would happen if you set yourself a time limit or did it standing up? Can you develop your speed reading skills, or just read the headline, intro and ending? Often I go straight to the last paragraph and, if it sounds intriguing, I will read more.

Know what you want, prioritise it, and be ruthless with the rest.

CHAPTER TWELVE

Underwhelming goals

"I don't try to jump over seven-foot bars. I look for one-foot bars that I can step over."

~ WARREN BUFFETT

In Chapter 5 you started to create your vision from the 'Dreamer' space. I suggested that you didn't do any initial editing or planning of how you would achieve your vision. I encouraged you to 'live with' your dreams without knowing how you would achieve them. In this section we get practical and I provide you with some tools to put sub-goals and plans in place. These plans serve several purposes. They provide you with a clear 'how to guide'. This can be especially useful when you're in 'the dip', and still want to make progress. They reduce the likelihood of you getting distracted.

Different people have different preferences around how to set and achieve goals. I suggest that in order to raise your game and achieve transformational results, it will be beneficial to change the way you set your goals. Many people set goals from the perspective of "from here, what's reasonable". I suggest that with your vision, you work backwards. Then it's only a matter of fitting it in. The art of working back includes creating a brain dump of everything that will need to be done and start to consider what can be started sooner. Essentially these are the skills of project management.

For example, if you're considering moving home or office – even if you don't yet have details or a timescale, there may be some de-cluttering of your existing home, or perhaps redecoration that can be planned in, or even beginning to define criteria for the new space.

If you are considering expanding your business, have you created role descriptions of the types of work you'd be looking for someone to do. Do you have a job advert ready to go? How clear are you on the criteria for hiring someone?

It seems that in order to be super effective we need both long-term and short-term goals. In order to write a book I found it useful to have the vision, and a goal of when I want to publish by ... as well as having specific weekly targets of both the number of hours I wanted to work on it – and in the initial stages – how many words I was aiming to write in one sitting.

After the initial euphoria has worn off, the end goal can seem a long way away. I mentioned in an earlier chapter that often any change can feel like failure in the middle. Having small targets or goals can be really useful when you hit that bit in the middle. At that time your vision might seem too large and overwhelming, so having the 'next' step clear and precise means that you'll have activities available in manageable sized chunks.

It's been said that we overestimate what we can achieve in one year and underestimate what we can achieve in ten years. So having a longer-term vision, which is sub-divided into range goals with different timescales, can be useful.

Many people's goal size is typically too big, and too far into the future. They don't set tiny goals that are related to their bigger goal.

Set underwhelming goals. Achieve a little and often. Be thrilled at your success on a daily basis rather than be disappointed at the end of the week. It doesn't take too many disappointments for people to 'give up' on their goals. Don't give up on your goals.

There are many books written about goals, effectiveness and efficiency. There are many ways to set goals. And if it was so easy then there'd be more people doing it! So then; I guess the question is: what stops us from setting and achieving our goals?

Discipline

We lack the discipline to do little and often, on a regular, consistent basis.

Distractions

Life certainly has a habit of presenting distractions and challenges, which can throw some people off course. These can be pleasant distractions of the "it's a nice afternoon, let's go to the pub by the river" variety. And challenges can be more unpleasant or serious; perhaps, learning of the admission into hospital of a close friend or relative, and rallying round to provide support.

If a person doesn't have a clear course or direction to start with – it's no wonder that these distractions can halt proceedings. It's much harder to "get back on track" if there was no clear track to start with.

Other people

Our commitments to others, who hold us accountable, seem to be more important than our own goals.

Have you ever found yourself supporting other people to achieve their goals to the detriment of your own? Often requests from friends and family sound innocuous enough. "Can you just ..." and there goes two hours of your time. There is always the option to say 'no' – although many people find this difficult. Saying 'no' breaks away from the norm. Stephen Covey suggests: "In order to say no, you need a burning yes." Your vision is your burning yes.

I'm not suggesting that you don't help; I am suggesting that you look at your commitments first and make a thought through decision, rather than a 'yes' that's based on a habitual response that you regret just moments after having made it.

It can be useful to be really clear about what's expected before you start, and to be clear about what you're prepared to give; perhaps, offer your time for a particular duration rather than until the end of the task. Should you wish, you can always go back and continue, and the break will ensure that you're also thinking and working on your priorities, and are not being side-tracked into working on someone else's vision to the detriment of your own.

One option is to trade time and skills. What skills are you providing them; what could they provide in return?

Rather than you dropping everything to do the task, perhaps you can postpone it ... find a more convenient time for you to do what's asked.

You could ask for time ... "I've got some other priorities this month. How long do you realistically think XYZ will take? Let me take a look at my diary and see when I could fit that in?"

Making decisions

I worked with a successful business director who suggested that one of the key skills that had brought him his early success was the ability to make a decision. He wasn't advocating quick decisions that weren't thought through. He would think about the information he needed in order to make the decision; he then set about gathering the appropriate information in order to make the decision, made the decision, and then moved on to the next thing. He said that he noticed people wasted a lot of time and mental energy NOT making the decision, especially where the decision involved people in the team.

It's useful to remember that we don't have crystal balls to see into the future – there will always be decisions that we make, that with hindsight and the benefit "of just a bit more information" we may not have made.

So how do you get the information in order to make decisions? There may be some obvious tangible information you need – and here's an approach my clients have found very useful, which makes some of the less tangible more tangible.

Outcome planning

Outcomes are things you want to achieve, as opposed to specific actions which are how you go about achieving them. For example, you might have an initial outcome of being fit with specific targets of weight. The actions will be around diet and exercise.

Many writers describe keeping the end goal very clear. This is a useful way of checking out whether you really want something – thinking through the effect on other aspects of your life (unlike *King Midas*), and checking that you're focusing your energies on things that are under your control.

Do you want it enough?

Some things are nice just as a dream – so how do you tell the difference between a dream and something you want to turn into reality? Some 'dreams' can be fun – and perhaps are not compelling enough that you actually want to do them.

> One corporate client I worked with had a dream to set up a cake baking shop. When she thought about the practicalities of doing it, she realised that although she enjoyed baking and decorating cakes for friends and family, she didn't want to turn it into a business. She liked the 'dream' but didn't want it to be her vision.

One way to think things through is an approach called outcome planning.

One problem is that often our dreams aren't specific enough – our brain seems to need the detail. Have you ever bought a new car … and only then does your brain start to notice other cars on the road that are exactly the same make / model / colour. It's almost like once primed with enough detail our brain says: "You want me to notice these … OK … there's one, there's another." So the trick is to tell your brain exactly what you're looking for so that it can help you find opportunities to make it happen.

Another example is the supermarket shop. When going to the supermarket some people take a list. The intention of the list is to guide decision making, and speed up the purchasing process. The list isn't a jumble of letters – the letters form words. When you have the words you create a representation in your head and when you see the physical item in the supermarket, you know it matches – 'bingo', success. It's the same with outcomes – they have to be specific in order that the brain knows what it's looking for.

It's a way of thinking through what you want, thinking through some of the implications. You might want to make a note of your answers for the record, to remind yourself why you chose (or didn't) your goals.

Over the next couple of pages are a comprehensive set of questions arranged in the following order:

- Get SMART with your outcome
- What resources do you need
- Dig into the sub-conscious
- What's stopping you
- How does it fit with your values
- Taking action!

Get SMART with your outcome

The way you define and describe your outcomes affects whether or not you achieve them.

Sometimes it can be hard to be objective when you're both asking and answering the questions, so I've created an audio file which contains the questions, so that you can focus on your answers. Download it from **raiseyourgame.biz**/download

Ask yourself the following:

1. What do I want? (The outcome.)
2. Is the outcome stated in the positive?
   If not, ask: "What would I like instead?"

If you hear yourself say what you don't want or it's about a loss (e.g. weight loss), then see if you can rephrase it to something that's positive. The brain doesn't process negatives very well. Notice what happens when I say: don't think about a blue donkey. For many people the image flashes up in their minds eye.

3. Is it specific enough? (Outcomes defined in a general way are less likely to be achieved.)

4. It may be useful to think about when, where, and with whom do I want it.

5. Is achieving this outcome under my control? (If it's not under my control – what is?)

   For example, if you were an athlete winning a gold medal is not under your control because you don't know what the other competitors will do 'on the day'. However putting in the necessary training to be in necessary shape to achieve a world record by the day of the Olympic event, is more within your control.

6. Is it the right size to be challenging and yet achievable? Check it's not too small for me to really care about or too big that it seems impossible?

7. How will I know when I have achieved it ... what will I see, hear and feel when I achieve my outcome?

8. What is it about me that will enable me to get it?

What resources do you need?

People often fail to achieve their outcomes because they do not acquire and use the resources that are needed for success, or because the 'knock-on' effects in their own and other people's lives make the outcomes seem unattractive, or because of the balance of priorities. The following questions test the achievability of the outcomes.

1. What resources do you need to achieve your outcome? E.g. personal qualities, experience, qualifications, interpersonal skills, self-confidence.

2. How will you get these resources? When?

3. How will you need to involve other people to help you achieve your outcome?

4. How will achieving your outcome affect other people?

5. What effect will it have on your life balance? What else would have to change or reorganise in order to achieve your outcome?

6. What benefit are you getting by staying the same?

7. What could you do to sabotage the achievement of your outcome? (Often we know what we do to conspire in us not achieving our goals!)

Dig into your sub-conscious

Odd questions

You might recognise these questions from Chapter 9, and the purpose of these carefully crafted questions is to scramble the conscious part of your brain to see what the sub-conscious 'pops-out'. There is no 'right' answer, your conscious brain can get busy with the logic, and just listen to the questions (read them as they're written) and notice what comes up for you!

1. What would happen if you did (do X)?

2. What would happen if you didn't (do X)?

3. What wouldn't happen if you did (do X)?

4. What wouldn't happen if you didn't (do X)?

What's stopping you?

For your outcome, **ask yourself**:

1. What stops me? -> limitation

2. What do I want instead (of this limitation)? -> outcome

3. Repeat ...
   Sometimes going through this process will evolve the outcome, or provide you with a set of tasks or sub goals.

Example: I want to work fewer hours.

- *What stops you?* - Too much work.
- *What do you want instead (of too much work)?* - Less work.
- *What stops you (having less work)?* - I sometimes take on too much.
- *What do you want instead (of taking on too much)?* - To be able to refuse work.
- *What stops you (refusing work)?* - Not knowing my ideal clients.
- *What do you want instead?*

... and so on

How does it fit with your values?

If you got this outcome what would it do for you? -> another outcome

If you got this outcome what would it do for you? -> yet another outcome

...and so on

Eventually you will get to a value! Typically, it will be one of your more important values. This may be a value that you recognise from Chapter 6; however, just occasionally it highlights a different value.

Or ask yourself:

- How do I know that my outcome is worth achieving?

Example: I want to stop working long hours.

- *If you got this outcome what would it do for you?* - I'd be less tired.
- *If you got this outcome (of being less tired) what would it do for you?* - I'd have more energy for my family.
- *If you got this outcome (of having more energy for your family) what would it do for you?* - I'd feel closer to them..
- *If you got this outcome (of feeling closer to them) what would it do for you?* - A good feeling, security (the value here is security).

If you find the value is different to those you found earlier, spend some time thinking about how it fits with your other values. This could be a cause of inner conflict that is taking your inner energy, and mental processing power, without you realising it.

As you come to the end of this process, you may realise that, like the 'cake shop lady', you don't want to pursue your goal and, if that's the case, it is back to the drawing board to design your vision. The good news is that you haven't wasted precious time, energy and resources on pursuing it.

However, having almost completed the process you might be really committed to proceed. You can check this by asking yourself: "On a scale of 1–10, how committed am I?"

(If the answer is anything less than a nine – follow up with the question … what has to happen to increase your commitment?

The process might also have highlighted specific sub goals or activities, and there are a final set of questions, which can sometimes be useful to get into action.

Taking action!

- What is your first step?
- When will you do it?
- Where will you do it?
- How will you do it?

I agree with the school of thought that says your next step should be within 24–48 hours to start momentum. This can be a very small step, like just booking time in your diary to do bigger steps – and there's a good feeling that comes with taking action.

Common mistakes in goal setting

Often it's easy to critique the goals of others – to notice the flaws in their thinking – it's harder to appraise our own goals.

 Many people give themselves too much 'wiggle room' when setting goals. Quite often, they don't want to be 'tied down', and don't want to fail – so they set their goals lightly, perhaps without clear timescales or, more typically, they don't set goals at all.

 Many people are too aggressive with their goal setting. The goal can quickly become seemingly insurmountable and therefore people give up at the first hurdle.

 Set underwhelming goals and overachieve.

 Many people give themselves excuses and let themselves off the hook far too easily. It's true that plans slip, but often people are 'distracted' or 'deluded' and don't have a clear focus on their priorities. If you find you never quite have the time to invest in your future … after all, it's a lovely afternoon and the grass does need mowing. If you recognise that type of distraction you're not holding yourself accountable – and there's no one else doing it for you.

 Hold yourself accountable

 Many people set goals that are outside of their control, and then quickly become disillusioned. I think this can happen if the link between input and output is not clear.

For example, one professional services client wanted an additional five clients in his portfolio by the end of the year. Typically of five prospects he would meet – four of them would not be immediately ready for his services. Therefore, in order to get five clients, he would need to create proposals for twenty prospects.

When he was in his Dreamer phase, and goal setting he found it too easy to forget the work involved. Even getting to the point of being invited to create twenty proposals involved a significant amount of work. Once he started to work on his plan he quickly became disillusioned at the sheer volume of the workload.

Whilst he can't make prospects become customers by forcing them to sign on the dotted line, he can ensure that he's getting in front of enough clients to make it likely that five will sign. Of course, there are additional things he might also look at, for example, to see if his conversion rate could be increased.

He knew the numbers, but when the first two prospects of his campaign didn't sign, it's too easy to slide into the dip. It feels like failure. When going into the dip, and you will, it's easier to sustain momentum if there are clear and simple targets of activity. For example, this week write to twenty business owners, of which four should invite a proposal (or tender), and of those at least one should convert to become a customer.

Sure, relax. Celebrate successes along the way. You should also celebrate effort.[37] Have small wins and celebrate them proportionally. Often external support can provide guidance to keep you on track and to check your goals.

Just one more step

Several years ago I was lucky enough to attend a corporate event with motivational speaker Chris Moon. Chris was blown up in Africa clearing landmines and lost his lower arm and leg. Inspirationally, less than a year after leaving hospital he completed the London Marathon, and subsequently went on to complete the Marathon des Sables. I heard Chris speak of his Marathon des Sables experience. The Marathon des Sables is a six-day / 151-mile (243-km) endurance race across the Sahara Desert in Morocco. This seems to me to be a real test of endurance even for those of us with all our limbs.

Chris described his experience, and the low point where he was exhausted, in pain, thirsty ... the question he would repeatedly ask was "can I take just one more step" ... and his answer was always yes. In these moments he was not looking towards the distance and the 'finish line' that was way over the horizon. His focus had become 'micro', the tiny next activities that kept his momentum going forward.

In this example the 'activity' is clear "just one more step"... in creating your transformational results – how clear are your small actions so that in the depth of the dip ... you can sustain your momentum.

Ask yourself:

● How clear are my next activities?

Critic

In terms of the Three Stage Thinking for Creativity, Chapter 5 covered Dreamer, the previous section covered Planner. You may find it strange that I'm not going to cover Critic in great detail.

Anticipate problems by asking yourself "what if" for a range of different scenarios. You'll no doubt quickly realise that this could become a mammoth task – and potentially unfocused and not that useful. So give yourself some structure, or work with someone who can provide a structured approach.

You will find that **if** you wish to share your vision with others, they will generally be generous in lavishing their opinions, and spotting any gaps in your thinking, and asking the what-if questions. Society's norm seems to delight in highlighting all the ways that something can't be done. With your growth mindset, you can take on-board their comments, and use them to make your plans even more robust. However, be single minded in your focus to achieve your vision and don't let others deflect you from it.

> *"Those that say it can't be done should get*
> *out of the way of those doing it."*
>
> **~ CHINESE PROVERB**

CHAPTER THIRTEEN

Best foot forward

"Appearances are not held to be a clue to the truth.
But we seem to have no other."

~ IVY COMPTON-BURNETT

Your appearance does matter

"You never get a second chance to make a first impression."

Many people are unaware that they miss opportunities
because of how they're dressed.

**Explore the topic of clothing, understand the
assumptions we make about each other based on how
we're dressed.**

Missing opportunities happens possibly more often than you realise
– *especially* if you think this topic is not relevant to you. Men, this
chapter is especially for you! Although women get image pushed
at them through the media, they're often given conflicting advice
– depending on whether viewed through the lens of this season's
fashion, and whether an outfit is slimming, or stylish. Therefore,
this chapter is relevant to both men and women.

I want to caveat this chapter by saying it's not a chapter on
fashion – so if you work in the fashion industry – this chapter is

not for you! This chapter is most relevant if when you meet people you represent a company, even if you consider that you're paid to use your brain. It's relevant if you provide a service, or if you've developed an asset.

> *"Fashion fades, only style remains the same."*
>
> ~ COCO CHANEL

You've heard it said that first impressions matter. Perhaps they shouldn't, but they do. Whilst it's true that your reputation does count – others subconsciously or consciously take in 'the whole package' of you, which includes how you look when they first meet you. Whether you admit it or not, everyone subconsciously takes in information about another person and forms an opinion.

If you want to test it, spend an hour in a coffee shop mid-week, mid-morning and 'people watch'. Notice who and what you're looking at and the assumptions that you make based on appearance. I'm not suggesting that it's good to form opinions or to make these assumptions, and without training you're probably making some form of judgement, whether or not you realise it. This activity is just a way to make the judgements you have about other people more explicit.

Sadly, there are so many examples where people talk behind someone's back about a person's appearance. For example, I overheard a conversation about a property investor with one person suggesting that "there's no way she'd get my money looking like that". I met a brilliant HR director; however, when she started in the role, she just didn't *look* like the HR director, and on meeting people initially had to overcome the impression that she's the *secretary* to the HR director. Never mind all the talking (and time wasting) that went on behind her back because of her slightly skimpy attire. This isn't just relevant to women. Indeed, it's probably more relevant to men. I've worked with a number of men who have been brilliant – but scruffy. Within the corporate world I've seen careers 'take-off' after taking image advice.

One reason that this talk happens behind backs is that it can be a difficult topic for people to know how discuss. If you're the leader, there are probably few people who can, or are willing to comment on your appearance. Even if your friends or family are aware of the impact you're having with your clothing, this can still be a difficult topic for friends to comment upon, as people take it personally. Be honest. Is there an aspect of one of your acquaintances' clothing that you would recommend they change? Have you said anything to them? What was the result? (If you haven't said anything, then why not?) There are several factors to take into account, for example: timing, sensitivity, specifics.

Let's take timing as an example. If your business partner arrived at an event inappropriately dressed – probably saying anything initially might put them ill at ease and you want them to be on top form – so you don't say anything. Then, by the time the event is over … 'the moment' to say something has passed, or may be taken badly, or in the grand scheme of things it doesn't seem important. I disagree; it's your reputation.

Often it's not something we talk about, so just as you wouldn't say something, others say nothing to you and therefore you may not be aware of the impact you're having. If you want to *raise your game* – you have to dress 'to the next level'. Take a look around at the respected people in your industry and take a moment to really notice how they're dressed. It's easy to think that they dress well *after* they've achieved success.

Sure there are exceptions – and it's almost like the *most* senior people can get away with a different image. I met a multi-millionaire brand builder with an awesome reputation, another poorly fitted suit, and in need of a hair-cut! His reputation precedes him, and you're broadening and building yours.

Common mistakes: not knowing how to dress 'smart casual'

 Smart casual does not mean casual.

 There is an appropriate way to dress for 'smart casual'.

Many people are surprised how 'formal' smart casual is. If you don't know what it is – you need to find out! A short summary is that for men it usually consists of a blazer or a sports jacket, a collared shirt, and smart trousers. Suits technically fall into the formal category, but some are casual enough to be considered smart casual. A tie is optional. Smart casual footwear includes shoes and loafers, but not trainers, or men's sandals. Knowing the 'smart casual' dress code is especially important if you ever go to external events such as conferences and you're likely to see prospects or clients.

For women there's a broader range of what's appropriate in smart casual. I think that women can 'get away with' a more casual approach – but there is something about being taken professionally that might mean as a woman you find that you dress more professionally in order to stand out and be taken seriously.

In a couple of paragraphs I talk more specifically about individual differences in body shape, and personality that will affect what you wear and how you wear it. "Booted and suited" is not for everyone.

If you lead others, then being aware that the impact you're having through what you wear is doubly important. Even if you believe that you're above the dress code, your team will look to you as the leader to set the standard, and they're taking cues off you. If you say smart casual, then turn up in casual, you will unwittingly confuse them. If you dress in a sloppy way, then don't be surprised if your team think that sloppy is an acceptable way to dress.

When you look around at others, if you're not familiar with the distinctions in clothing, you may only notice that someone is wearing jeans. Don't be fooled. If you've ever tried to buy simply 'a pair of jeans', you will know there are differences. There are also different ways to wear jeans, from the low slung ways of the youth, to the low slung ways of the builder's jeans. To you it might just be jeans, and jeans can be 'dressed up' to smarter casual with smart shoes, good quality belt, shirt and jacket, or 'dressed down' to a more weekend casual look. It's OK not to give a damn about clothes – and make sure you take appropriate advice.

Making your clothing work for you

This is not about what you feel comfortable wearing, that's based on what you've worn up to now. This is about the unconscious signals your clothing gives to others. The impression you want to give is that you take yourself seriously, you invest in yourself, and you are therefore of interest to others who may want to invest their time in speaking to you – or make a more tangible investment in your business.

Some people lack awareness around professional image and think that putting a suit on is smart enough. However, perhaps they don't realise that it's poorly fitted. They ruin the look further with bulging pockets, an inappropriate belt and 'wrong' shoes – and at an extreme – a poor quality shirt. Paying more doesn't automatically guarantee a good fit, style or colour.

Give yourself a quick appearance assessment – if you think that you might lack awareness, you may want to enlist someone to give you some direct feedback. Rate yourself out of five, where one is poor, and five is you maintain a super high standard.

	Respected person in your industry	You
Hair		
Glasses		
Tie		
Jewellery		
Make-up		
Jacket		
Trousers / fit / length		
Skirt / dress		
Socks / hosiery		
Shoes		

Accessories

Watch		
Briefcase / handbag		
Pen		
Notebook		
Wallet / Purse		

After you've done the image audit, and you've been very honest with yourself, you might have found that it's time for an image upgrade. My strong recommendation to you is: DON'T hit the shops alone!

Find an image consultant

Find an image consultant. Some large department stores provide free clothing advisors. Don't do this. Store based advisors typically make recommendations based on the available stock, which is based on this season's fashion colours and styles – which may not be what works for you in terms of colour or shape. These guys provide a great service, after you know what suits you.

For your initial consultation I recommend that you see someone independent of a store. There are a couple of franchises in the UK that offer image consultancy: House of Colour and Colour Me Beautiful. They both do similar things.

What does an image consultant do?

They look at your skin and hair colouring – and work out the colours that suit you. They look at your body shape and your proportions and work out clothing styles and cut most likely to flatter you whatever this season's trend. Often they include an element of matching clothing to personality when they provide their guidelines to you.

The colours that suit you may not necessarily be ones that you like or that you've ever worn before – and these colours will ensure that you look your best, not washed out, drained or tired. They also take time to describe specific differences around different dress codes: between formal, business formal, business casual and casual, and appropriate accessories for each.

The advantage is a simplified wardrobe, knowing what clothing is appropriate for which situation, and often this simplified wardrobe provides things that just 'work' together. Here are some common objections and my responses.

I can't be bothered by clothes or shopping – why would I do this?

Over time – an investment in image consultancy can save you time shopping.

Many people don't enjoy the shopping experience, or they're time poor and want to ensure they get maximise value from the time they spend shopping. Indeed, for some people there's always something more important to do than to shop for clothes – then this is exactly the reason I suggest that you invest in seeing an image consultant who very very quickly will save you time.

I love shopping for clothes; won't this detract from my experience

Some people love the shopping experience – and knowing some detail around what suits you best will add a new dimension to your shopping experience. Within the guidelines there's still plenty of room to be creative. You can look for unusual pieces, *and* you still have the ability to combine items in interesting ways, to add your unique sense of flair and panache – this doesn't get taken away.

Going the full nine yards

Additional services by these image consultants or *diva's of the wardrobe* include a wardrobe clear out – finding the pieces that you already own that really work for you – and the voice of reason to encourage you to discard (perhaps to a charity shop) the remaining items that are doing you no favours.

With a pared down wardrobe and knowledge of what you need – I highly recommend a trip to the shops with one of these divas. If you don't normally do a big clothes shop it can seem expensive to buy everything in one go – and at the end of the trip you should have a range of clothes and accessories that *work* for you, knowledge of how to put them together – and specific guidance for how to do it again in the future.

I don't want to be a clone!

One objection I hear is "I don't want to be a clone". This hasn't been my experience for two main reasons: firstly, the sheer number of combinations. Broadly speaking, there are four main colourings and at least six different body shapes. That alone gives 24 different combinations – and that's without including the element of personality or some more subtle nuances around colour and body shape and proportions.

But I like black

It's true that there are advantages to wearing black, and advantages to having a wardrobe with a predominance of black items. Black is easy to match with other black items. Apparently it has magical slimming properties. It doesn't draw too much attention to you, and I understand that there are several professions which require wearing black. Not least of all funeral directors.

However, there are relatively few people who suit wearing the colour black. It's a sombre colour, and typically lacks flair and imagination. For most people it has a draining effect on their skin tone. Black absorbs light. It absorbs the colour from your skin, often leaving people looking washed out and drained. There are plenty of other dark colours; your image consultant will work with you to find one which you will look even better in.

Not everyone will judge me on my appearance

It's true that not everyone will judge you (either consciously or unconsciously) on your appearance, and why take the risk? You want to raise your game – you want to increase your impact and increase the likelihood of people saying 'yes' to your proposals and propositions. Why risk them saying 'no' or worse still, not having the opportunity to speak to them in the first place because of some prejudice around the shoes that you wear – or your matching *Mickey Mouse* socks and tie that your kids bought you last summer and that you wear for sentimental reason. Sure break the rules – and first know what they are.

I can't afford it (yet)

Many people think: "When I've achieved the next success ... then I'll invest in ..." Like many aspects in life, investment comes before results. Image is a factor which will contribute to your success, so find a way to do it, even if initially it's on a budget. The French and Italians spend a much higher percentage of their earnings on clothing than us Brits. Within the corporate sector the advice is to invest at least 10% of your salary each year on clothing. This can make a big impact not least of all because with guidance many of your pieces will be timeless – apart from wear and tear – your investment will grow.

For the initial investment, I recommend the individual one-to-one day with an image consultant. However, an alternative is the cheaper group session. Typically they offer separate group sessions for colour and body shape. Although cheaper it's more of your precious time on a topic which may not be of interest – and if it's something you think you'll enjoy – luxuriate in the one-to-one experience.

Once you've made the initial investment, updating your image needn't be costly, and the clothes in your wardrobe will work together, so over the long term it's likely that you will save money. With good foundation pieces you'll find it much easier to mix and match.

Investing in your image needn't be costly; it can be done bit by bit. Let's take an example of getting a decent pen. If you don't have one, then pens probably aren't 'your thing', which is fine, and other people will notice. Sure you could get an expensive brand name pen – and there are nice looking pens that are far more reasonably priced. And if you hear yourself saying "but I'm not the type of person who ..." then revisit Chapter 7.

Elevator pitch

Another aspect of presenting yourself and putting your best foot forward is about how you introduce yourself and your ideas.

Many people can't answer clearly the question: "What do you do?"

Be able to introduce yourself and what you do clearly and succinctly.

Too often I meet people who are not able to say what they do or the opportunities that they're looking for. Sometimes this is down to wanting to keep their options open, and to maximise the likelihood of someone using their skills and wanting their services. At other times it can be their own lack of clarity on what they want next, never mind what they want to be doing in five or ten years' time.

There can be a fear of arrogance of not wanting to blow your own trumpet. However, it's hard to make introductions or connections with someone when it's not clear what they do or they're so broad in their approach.

Don't be modest, and don't over aggrandise. Whilst you may 'get away with' hyping up an idea once, over time your credibility will diminish, as people constantly take what you say with a pinch of salt. When you hype things up, whatever outcome you suggest, others mentally reduce or ignore it. You probably value long-term relationships – so be sure that you don't fall into the trap of 'crying wolf'.

You have between 30 seconds to 90 seconds to convey your answer the question 'what do you do?' and build interest. You might have clever expressions or fancy terminology, and do the majority of people understand them? Be succinct and clear and a conversation will follow. What do you say? Record it, and listen to it. Get some honest feedback, either from friends or family, from new acquaintances at networking groups or from your mentor or coach. When you've got your vision set, it's important to be able to articulate clearly and concisely what you do. Ensure that the impression you convey is the one you want to be remembered for.

CHAPTER FOURTEEN

Your travel guide

"You get the best effort from others not by lighting a fire beneath them, but by building a fire within."

~ **BOB NELSON**

An unreasonable friend to keep you moving forward

Increasing your goals by an order of magnitude is likely to involve some stretching. Stretching will take you outside your comfort zone, which by definition will be uncomfortable. In these moments of discomfort, it can often feel easier to turn back, and to retreat to comfort. Turning back will not take you towards the transformational results that you seek. In these moments it can be really useful to have what I describe as an unreasonable friend to provide support, discipline and encouragement.

Who do you answer to? Do you have 'wiggle room' to get out of agreements? I'm talking here about commitments you make to yourself. You probably keep your commitments to other people *because* they're looking at you, and keeping you accountable (perhaps their version is to make you feel guilty). Do you always do what you set out to do for yourself?

Before looking at who might fulfil the role of an unreasonable friend, let's look at some of the things you'll be asking of them.

The qualities that you're looking for in an unreasonable friend

For an unreasonable friend to provide support to you, you'll probably wish to share your dreams, your vision for the future as well as specific goals. It's therefore essential that you trust them and that you know what you say will remain confidential.

An unreasonable friend is likely to have qualities that you respect, and they may have a different 'values system'. You will be growing and developing and your thinking will change. You want someone who can support you through this change – it's likely that they too will have been on this journey of change and experienced some of the ups and downs along the way. Check they have time to support you in your journey.

I'm sure the expression *swimming in treacle* must come from someone experiencing change and growth. As with any new skill, it takes time to learn, and more time to master. In order to support you, your unreasonable friend needs a good combination of patience, encouragement and the ability to hold you accountable. They need to have awareness of what you do, and also to understand the impact it might have on others, and the ability to provide appropriate unbiased feedback, or direction or support, depending on what's needed!

In turn they have to have earned your respect so that you'll listen to their feedback, and agree to being held accountable by them.

Celebrate your successes

Your unreasonable friend will ensure you celebrate your successes without feeling jealous because they will have had plenty of their own successes.

Encourage you through the dip

Sometimes it's necessary to "put on a brave face", and with your unreasonable friend – you have to be willing to "let them in", so that they can support you when you're facing the dip and encourage you to make small manageable steps to help you through, and maintain momentum.

Your unreasonable friend must also be able to see when you're cruising – and to be able to encourage you to increase your own challenge.

Hold you accountable

Most people lack consistent self-discipline. They don't do what they say they're going to do.

Find ways of being accountable to yourself. Don't let yourself down!

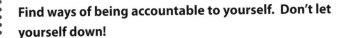

Whilst celebrating success is great, often what we dislike has a disproportionate impact on us. In Chapter 8 I gave the example of the cockroach in the bowl of cherries. This applies here too. Your unreasonable friend will work with you to set appropriate challenges and you'll agree what penalties there are for non-compliance. They will hold you to your commitments. Celebrating success with a bottle of champagne or in whatever way you decide is great ... and what if you set yourself a penalty for non-achievement of your goals. Given that you work for yourself, you won't be sacked – and how much more likely would it be for you to achieve your big goals if by non-achievement you knew you'd have to 'give up' a luxury of importance to you.

Your unreasonable friend has to have strength of character and hold you accountable for non-achievement of goals and commitments. You are a determined person – they must be as equally determined to stand up to you, to not fear confrontation with you, to work with you to set consequences. You know that not everyone can do that.

The ability to listen

They have to be able to listen to you, to hear what you say – and importantly to hear what you're not saying.

Who is this unreasonable friend?

Who can you enlist to be your 'unreasonable friend' with super high expectations of you, that cheers you on when you're successful, supports you when you're low, and doesn't let you wheedle out of commitments, especially the ones you make to yourself?

 Many people either don't have, or choose someone inappropriate to be their unreasonable friend.

First of all I'll explore some common mistakes that people make when selecting someone to be their unreasonable friend.

Existing friend: perhaps you think an unreasonable friend is a role that can be performed by an existing friend. Consider the strain on the relationship if they can hold you accountable at inappropriate times. You'll find yourself more frustrated by them than supported by them. Perhaps your friends hold your secrets, but an on-going relationship of accountability can be a 'big ask' and something which is ultimately a burden on your friend, and will change the nature of your relationship. You're asking them to be slightly duplicitous – to be in the company of others and to sometimes withhold information they know about you. By all means keep them as trusted advisors, and informal buddies.

Partner: in the same vein, you might think that your partner (husband / wife) can provide this support – hopefully they'll be supportive of you anyway! It can be hard for a partner to turn off emotions; they're emotionally involved with you even if they are not involved with your business. They're not detached enough from you, your business or your decisions to be independent.

In addition, there's an important balance between spending time with your family verses your focus on raising your game. Even if your partner is involved in the business, it's important to have an organisation chart in place to be clear who makes the final decisions.

Business Partner: when things are going well a business partner can be great to bounce ideas around with, and sometimes some fresh thinking is what's needed. If goals become out of alignment between you and your business partner it can cause a reluctance to share – which can cause a greater rift in the relationship than is necessary.

Mentor: a mentor is someone who had been on the journey that you're going on, who has more knowledge than you and is willing to impart their wisdom. Often mentoring is voluntary, fairly loose and done on ad-hoc basis. You could consider putting a more formal agreement in place about how to progress the relationship. There are some questions to ask: can they support you to run your own race? And they don't just want you to copy their advice, perhaps as a boost to their ego? How skilled is your mentor in supporting you? Do they know where they are in relation to the stages of change (conscious competence) ... and do they remember the struggles they went through?

Some business mentoring operates on a more formal basis – and is more akin to business coaching – described more fully below.

Another Business Person: you might know a fellow business person where you can provide mutual support; however, you're looking for a business person who's already successful and / or active in growing their business. Check they'll have time to support you when you need it the most. This person could be ideal to engage as part of your team of trusted advisors, or your Master Mind group.[38]

Raise your Game

If you want to raise your game I strongly recommend that you find yourself external support, specifically some form of coaching. Many successful people hire an external coach to support and hold them accountable.

I am a coach specialising in behavioural change. I work with small numbers of individuals on a one-to-one basis, and groups who want to change their behaviours – it's an area I've specialised in over the past decade.

I have a fifteen-session *"raise your game"* coaching framework, which is specifically focused on raising your game. I'd be delighted for you to contact me at raiseyourgame.biz to find out more about the programs that I offer.

In order to get results, my programmes are a mix of training, coaching, and support – almost everything you need to change behaviours in a lasting way ... that last bit of magic – the commitment has to come from you.

However, you have other choices of external support, which may be more appropriate. For business owners, business coaching is a great option – with the focus on increasing your business bottom line, giving you more time and less stress.

Business coaching

An important element of business coaching is the focus on your business results. Business coaches are typically skilled professionals. A qualified business coach brings a wealth of business experiences, tools and methodologies for how to improve all aspects of your business, from increasing the numbers of prospects, turning them into customers, and improving profitability. Business coaches have skills and tools in sales and marketing, finance, people management, and systemising your business, and as well as a set of coaching skills, they also provide a training and mentoring element.

Check your coach's business experience; do they have knowledge and systems to impart to improve your business. A short checklist of questions is: do you think they will be an effective coach? Are they robust enough to hold you accountable? Are they part of a system? Do they get their own coaching or supervision?

Whilst there are many good independent business coaches – you might find it useful for a business coach to be connected to a broader network of contacts, systems and approaches. A business coach typically only takes on one client in a particular industry, in a particular geographic area at any one time. An independent business coach may not have experience of your industry – a business coach that's part of a network of other coaches will be able to speak with other business coaches in your industry to find ideas of 'what's worked' in other locations.

Business coaches differ from business consultants in that typically consultants are hired to do a specialist piece of work. Consultants come in, do the work, and leave without either coaching or developing your skills. For example, if IT is not your core business, a consultant might come in to your business, scope and implement the IT system. Although you will have got involved in providing the initial brief, you don't need to get involved in the physical set-up.

All you need is to ensure that you and your team have the skills to use the system post implementation.

The business coach provides knowledge, skills and processes to the business owner, alongside coaching and accountability so that you can enhance both your current and future businesses. After all, you probably won't stop when this business is complete, because you've got the entrepreneurial bug and also know the risks of not having the next goal in place!

You might be wondering about the investment needed to hire a business coach. For individual business coaching, at the low end the investment is £1000 for a couple of sessions per month, through to £2500 and beyond. This isn't about an hourly rate; but for their involvement with your business, and ensuring you get the resulting business outcomes you are seeking.

Working with an experienced business coach, it is likely that there will be some quick wins within the first couple of months (during this time they can find their fee in savings or new business). However, if you're serious about having some transformational results, then you're probably looking at an initial intensive twelve-month commitment, often followed by a less frequent on-going relationship – and that depends on how high you're aiming!

What about life coaches?

The coaching profession is not well regulated. Pretty much anyone can set up as a 'life coach'. Life coaches tend to work with the personal side of things, and in particular circumstances may be very useful. Some coaches are also qualified counsellors or therapists, and are regulated through their profession. There is also a new field of what are described as 'personal consultants', which offers a combination of therapy, and coaching, exploring both what holds you back and coaching you to move forward. Each of these types of coaches are more likely to practice the pure form of coaching – which is focused on asking questions. Life coaches do not provide suggestions.

Questions are great, and sometimes we need suggestions, fresh insights – and knowing that your business coach has extensive business experience and knowledge and is willing to provide a 'sanity check' for your ideas can be reassuring.

Whichever type of external support you're considering; there are some common concerns that people have.

I should know this

Firstly, who says that you 'should' know this? Whilst I agree that none of the concepts are particularly challenging to understand, there is a difference between knowledge and application or implementation. You've formed habits over a number of years, generally because they work. However, when you're trying to change the way you do things, remember that there are many 'forces' which have a strong pull for you to maintain the status quo, and to not change, and some of these forces may be within your current support network. It's therefore useful to have a pull or some external support to support you in making changes, encouraging you to *raise your game*.

I should be able to do all this myself

- Thinking: *"I should be able to do this myself".*

- *"No man is an island"* ~ **John Donne**

Whilst you might have all the skills, it can be enormously useful to have an unreasonable friend or coach to bounce ideas off and who hold you accountable. Look around – successful people don't do it alone, they have a band of advisors.

I'm too [old, young] to do this

Change is possible, and in the words of Henry Ford: "Whether you think you can, or whether you think you can't you're right." The steps to Raise your Game are effective, whether you're taking the first faltering steps, or are a more experienced traveller, you might want an unreasonable friend to support you on your journey.

That's a big investment

The statistic that is most striking is that firms that invest in training are significantly less likely to close than those that do not.[39] Invest for transformational results. Remember that an investment should provide more in returns than your initial investment.

Some of this is 'fluffy stuff'

If you're not ready to raise your game then coaching may not be for you, as coaching's not for everyone. However, I'm guessing that as you've read this far, you realise the huge importance of some of the 'soft skills' and habits I've introduced. You also know that obstacles that can get in the way of achieving transformational results can be a combination of business and personal. I described business coaching, and the tangible business results that business coaches get for their clients. I have a strong business background, and my specialist focus is working with clients on their 'mind game'. I deliver behavioural change, both one-to-one, and in groups. I offer a fifteen-session programme, which takes clients through the mind game and focuses on raising their personal game. To find out more, contact me on ***raiseyourgame.biz***

I wish you success in raising your game and achieving transformational results. I would be delighted for you to share your success on **raiseyourgame.biz**.

"To your success!"

References

"Standing on the shoulders of giants."

[1] Ryan, Richard M., & Deci, Edward L (2000). Self-determination theory and the facilitation of intrinsic motivation, social development, and well-being. *American Psychologist, 55*(1), 68-78. doi: 10.1037/0003-066x.55.1.68

[2] Csikszentmihalyi, Mihaly (2002). *Flow : the classic work on how to achieve happiness* (Rev. ed. ed.). London: Rider.

[3] Ariely, Dan (2008). *Predictably irrational : the hidden forces that shape our decisions*. [New York]: HarperCollins.

[4] Collins, James C (2001). *Good to great : why some companies make the leap – and others don't*. London: Random House Business.

[5] Godin, Seth (2007). *The dip : the extraordinary benefits of knowing when to quit (and when to stick)*. London: Piatkus.

[6] King, Laura A (2001). The hard road to the good life: The happy, mature person. *Journal of Humanistic Psychology, 41*(1), 51-72. doi: 10.1177/0022167801411005

[7] Coyle, Daniel (2009). *The talent code : unlocking the secret of skill in maths, art, music, sport, and just about everything else*. London: Random House.

[8] Dweck, Carol S (2006). *Mindset : the new psychology of success*. New York: New York : Random House.

[9] Blackwell, Lisa S., Trzesniewski, Kali H., & Dweck, Carol Sorich (2007). Implicit Theories of Intelligence Predict Achievement Across an Adolescent Transition: A Longitudinal Study and an Intervention. *Child Development, 78*(1), 246-263. doi: 10.1111/j.1467-8624.2007.00995.x

[10] Collins (see 4).

[11] Pink, Daniel H (2008). *A whole new mind : why right-brainers will rule the future* (New ed. ed.). London: Marshall Cavendish Business.

[12] Rooke, David, & Torbert, William R (2005). Seven Transformations of Leadership. *Harvard Business Review.*

[13] Lyubomirsky, Sonja (2010). *The how of happiness : a practical approach to getting the life you want.* London: Piatkus.

[14] Hill, Napoleon (2009). *Think and grow rich* ([New] ed. / [with an introduction by Tom Butler-Bowdon]. ed.). Chichester: Capstone.

[15] Taylor, Shelley E., Pham, Lien B., Rivkin, Inna D., & Armor, David A (1998). Harnessing the imagination: Mental simulation, self-regulation, and coping. *American Psychologist, 53*(4), 429-439. doi: 10.1037/0003-066x.53.4.429

[16] Kappes, Heather Barry, & Oettingen, Gabriele (2011). Positive fantasies about idealized futures sap energy. *Journal of Experimental Social Psychology, 47*(4), 719-729. doi: 10.1016/j.jesp.2011.02.003

[17] Schwartz, Shalom (2005). Basic Human Values: An Overview. Retrieved 18th August, 2012, from http://www.unienna.it/scienzepsicologiche/doc/tirocinio/Schwartz_paper.pdf

[18] Beck, Don, & Cowan, Christopher C. (2006). *Spiral dynamics : mastering values, leadership and change : explaining the new science of memetics.* Oxford: Blackwell.

Or see http://spiraldynamics.org/learning/Intro_to_SD.pdf

[19] Gerber, Michael E (1995). *The E-myth revisited : why most small businesses don't work and what to do about it.* New York, N.Y.: HarperBusiness.

[20] Simms, Andrew, & Woodward, David (2006). Growth isn't Working. nef. Retrieved 18th August, 2012, from http://www.neweconomics.org/sites/neweconomics.org/files/Growth_Isnt_Working_1.pdf

[21] Adapted from Dilts' Neurological Levels.

[22] Fredrickson, Barbara (2009). *Positivity : groundbreaking research reveals how to embrace the hidden strength of positive emotions, overcome negativity, and thrive* (1st ed.). New York: Crown Publishers.

[23] Kahneman, Daniel (2011). *Thinking, fast and slow.* London: Allen Lane. (p. 302) an example from Paul Rozin

[24] Kahneman, Daniel (2011). *Thinking, fast and slow.* London: Allen Lane.

[25] Chabris, Christopher F., & Simons, Daniel J (2010). *The invisible gorilla : and other ways our intuitions deceive us* (1st ed. ed.). New York: Crown.

Hood, Bruce (2012). *The Self Illusion.* UK: Constable & Robinson Ltd.

Kahneman, (see 24)

[26] Schwartz, Tony, Gomes, Jean, & McCarthy, Catherine (2010). *The way we're working isn't working : the four forgotten needs that energize great performance.* London: Simon & Schuster.

[27] Seligman, Martin E. P., & Csikszentmihalyi, Mihaly (2000). Positive psychology: An introduction. *American Psychologist, 55*(1), 5-14. doi: 10.1037/0003-066x.55.1.5 Also, Lyubomirsky (see 13).

[28] Lyubomirsky (see 13).

[29] Zimbardo, Philip G., & Boyd, John (2008). *The time paradox : the new psychology of time.* London: Rider.

[30] Reivich, Karen, & Shatté, Andrew (2002). *The resilience factor : 7 essential skills for overcoming life's inevitable obstacles* (1st ed.). New York: Broadway Books.

[31] Gilbert, Dan (2004). Why are we happy? Why aren't we happy? Retrieved 26th July, 2011, from http://www.youtube.com/watch?v=LTO_dZUvbJA

[32] Kahneman, (see 24)

[33] Adair, John Eric (1990). *The art of creative thinking.* Guildford: Talbot Adaair Press.

[34] UK Commission for Employment and Skills (2010). Encouraging small firms to invest in training: learning from overseas: Praxis. Retrieved 18th August, 2012, from http://www.ukces.org.uk/assets/ukces/docs/publications/praxis-5-encouraging-small-firms-to-invest-in-training.pdf

[35] Cooperrider, David L., & Whitney, Diana Kaplin (2005). *Appreciative inquiry : a positive revolution in change* (1st ed. ed.). San Francisco, CA: Berrett-Koehler.

[36] Covey, Stephen R (1989). *The seven habits of highly effective people : restoring the character ethic.* London: Simon & Schuster, 1992.

[37] Dweck (see 8).

[38] Hill (see 14).

[39] UK Commission for Employment and Skills (see 36).

About the author

Suzanne has a deep desire to help others "be the best they can", which inspires her to bring her mix of business experience, coaching and training to a wider audience. It is Suzanne's firm desire that readers discover and use these simple techniques, in order to start their upward spiral to success and fulfilment.

Suzanne is a coach specialising in behavioural change within business. Suzanne has trained or coached more than 3500 people either in small group sessions or in one-to-one coaching and regularly delivers conference workshops. Suzanne has worked nationally and internationally, including US, South Africa, Denmark, Netherlands, France and Germany.

Her interest in professional development spans two decades. After a first degree in Industrial and Business Systems and an early career in IT, which encompassed project and people management, for the past ten years, enabling others has been a full time vocation and passion for Suzanne. For seven years within IBM, Suzanne specialised in developing and delivering personal development training courses, before founding her own business.

Suzanne is a practitioner in a number of inter-related approaches such as: NLP (MPrac), Firo-B, and the Myers-Briggs Type Indicator (MBTI). She's taken advanced training in psychotherapy and more recently has successfully completed a Master's degree in Applied Positive Psychology (MAPP), and is excited to bring the findings to a wider audience. Suzanne holds coaching qualifications, and is an associate member of the Coaching Division of the British Association of Counselling and Psychotherapy (BACP), a member of the International Positive Psychology Association (IPPA) and is a trained business coach, now based in Surrey.

Testimonials

"This book is a MUST-READ for any successful business owner that is stuck in a rut! The problem is, most business owners that are in a rut, are either in denial, or unaware that there is so much more that they could be, do, have and give in life. Are you really living life to your true potential or have you settled for less? If you want to raise your game and re-discover how to live life to the full and love what you do, you must read this book!"

Steve Bolton,
Founder, Platinum Property Partners and President of Peace One Day Patrons

"Raise Your Game is a breath of fresh air in the massively over-populated genre of self-help business books. Whether you are someone who wants to be a successful entrepreneur, or someone who is working for an existing organisation - large or small - this book is something you should read...and then read again. Written in an easily digestible style, Raise Your Game could very well be the book that can help you realise your potential."

Dr. James B. Rieley,
Organisational Strategist, Systems Thinker and Author

"Ideal for the busy entrepreneur, this book is a superb and easily accessible reference library packed with strategies and tactics to help you reconnect to your vision and stretch and reach new levels"

Kevin Whelan,
Economist and Founder of The Kingswood Law Group

"Raise your game is a distillation of reams of relevant research with key small ingredients added in, which blend brilliantly to make a big difference to the outcomes you get. Suzanne Hazelton has the rare gift of being able to break down complex theory into simple and easy to follow actions that will transform your life.

Enjoy the application and the results."

Ian Christelow,
Managing Director, ActionCOACH

Contact Details

QR Code for website

My blog is **www.suzannehazelton.com**

Find me on Twitter: **https://twitter.com/suzannehazelton**

For downloads and further information about coaching programmes, the website is: **www.raiseyourgame.biz**

See more about my professional credentials on LinkedIn: **uk.linkedin.com/in/suzannehazelton**

To contact me for a no obligation discussion, email me at: **Suzanne@thebusinessofchange.co.uk**